The Most Estimable Of Men
Judge John O'Hagan
Patriot, Poet, Scholar, Lawyer

Thomas J. Morrissey SJ

Messenger Publications,
37 Leeson Place, Dublin D02 E5V0
www.messenger.ie

TABLE OF CONTENTS

Part One (1822–55):
Early Years, Young Irelander, Lawyer

Part Two (1856–90):
Educator, High Court Judge, Poet

John O'Hagan 1850

ACKNOWLEDGEMENTS

Many people have been most helpful in the publication of this book, particularly Damien Burke of the Irish Jesuit archives, Noelle Dowling of the Dublin Diocesan archives, and the archivist and staff of the University College Dublin archives.

My thanks are also due to Peter Beirne of the Clare County Library, who was most helpful in tracing John O'Hagan's legal career in that county; Dr Teresa Whitington, Librarian at the Catholic Central Library, for her assistance with John Henry Newman's correspondence; Dr Mary Esther Clarke, who provided me with copies of O'Hagan's obituaries; Kieran Rankin of The Statistical and Social Inquiry Society of Ireland; Judge Mary Finlay Geoghegan and Renate Ní Uigin, Librarian at King's Inns, Dublin, for their efforts in providing copies of O'Hagan's portraits; and the Abbess of the Convent of St Clare Sisters, Drumshanbo, County Leitrim, for information and correspondence concerning O'Hagan's widow.

A special word of appreciation to Patrick Carberry SJ, the careful and challenging reader of the text, who has done so much to improve this work. It remains for me to thank the members of my community at Milltown Park, Dublin, for their ongoing support, and the Jesuit provincial, Fr Leonard Moloney, for his assistance and encouragement. Finally, may I express once again my appreciation of the professional skill and courtesy of the editor and staff of Messenger Publications.

Thomas J. Morrissey SJ

INTRODUCTION

John O'Hagan's name is known to very few today, yet he was a man of many gifts who, in his youth as well as in later life, was greatly admired, even revered, by his contemporaries. Two centuries later, his life, work and values still have a contemporary resonance.

As a Catholic youth of fifteen, O'Hagan entered Trinity College, Dublin University, in 1837, graduating with a BA degree five years later. As an undergraduate, he became active in the College Historical Society, in which members of the Young Ireland Party were prominent. Recently founded in the College, the Young Irelanders were committed to promoting a knowledge of Irish history and eliciting pride in it. They supported Daniel O'Connell[1] in his campaign for repeal of the political union with Great Britain. They were also conscious of being part of a greater movement, the transition from an aristocratic to a democratic society, that was then taking place in the Western world. Impressed by the Young Irelanders, O'Hagan joined their ranks and became an ardent nationalist.

Among the Young Irelanders were several people destined to achieve renown as promoters of Irish independence. Thomas Davis[2] was the leading spirit and most admired member of the movement.

---

1 Daniel O'Connell (1775–1847) was an Irish lawyer and orator, and leader of the movement to obtain Catholic Emancipation. With the success of this movement in 1829, he and his elected followers were entitled to take part in the British parliament, where they were active in promoting reform and benefits for Ireland. In 1840, he set out on a campaign for the restoration of an Irish parliament. (The earlier Irish parliament had been submerged in the Act of Union with Great Britain, which came into force on 1 January 1801). O'Connell was unsuccessful in this attempt.
2 Thomas Davis (1814–1845), from Mallow, County Cork, was the most able and revered member of the Young Irelanders, who sought to unify Protestant and Catholics in one political movement. As a poet, writer and leading figure in the success of *The Nation* newspaper, he remained modest and self-effacing. He died at age of thirty.

Charles Gavan Duffy[3] was editor of *The Nation* newspaper, which made Young Ireland known throughout the country, and was later an advocate of revolution. Other members included John Blake Dillon, John Mitchel, William Smith O'Brien, Thomas Francis Meagher and other names familiar to students of Irish history.

In this pantheon of notable figures involved in Irish political reform and revolution, O'Hagan received little attention in the written history of the time, so that he is virtually unknown to posterity. Nevertheless, his influence was felt in the movement itself and in the years that followed. Speaking of the young O'Hagan, Gavan Duffy wrote that, despite 'a boyish face, a frank smile and a readiness to engage in badinage', he had a maturity beyond his years and was 'the safest in council, the most moderate in opinion, the most considerate in temper, of the young men,' so that, 'after a time, any of them would have recourse to him, next after Davis, in a personal difficulty needing sympathy and discretion'.[4]

Further witness comes from O'Hagan's friend and fellow student of law in London, John Pigot, who wrote of him: 'Who could spend so many evenings with such a friend without being the better morally and intellectually? He is just my own age, yet there are few men to whom I feel myself more entirely inferior … He has perhaps read less books than I, but he has thought more … He did me a great deal of good … by his deeper and clearer reason … but how much more good by the example of his religion. More than I can ever sufficiently

3   Charles Gavan Duffy (1816–1903), was born in County Monaghan. He was a journalist, editor, poet and politician. A Young Irelander, he promoted the 1848 rising. Following further involvement in Irish politics, he later emigrated to Australia, where he was elected Premier of Victoria. He wrote a history of the Young Ireland movement.

4   Gavan Duffy, Young Ireland: A fragment of history, 1840–1850 (Dublin: M. H. Gill & Son, 1884), (1896 ed.), p. 133.3 John Pigot, 'Memorandum', cited by Matthew Russell in *Irish Monthly*, February 1903, p. 65. Pigot himself was a prominent member of the Young Ireland movement, and later a significant figure in the world of art and culture.

5   John Pigot, 'Memorandum', cited by Matthew Russell in *Irish Monthly*, February 1903, p. 65. Pigot himself was a prominent member of the Young Ireland movement, and later a significant figure in the world of art and culture.

thank him for.'[5]

O'Hagan's close friend, Denis Florence MacCarthy, himself a poet, had O'Hagan in mind when writing his lengthy poem 'A Lay Missioner'. Towards the end he summarised his friend's character thus:

Such is my friend, and such I fain would be,
Mild, thoughtful, modest, faithful, loving, gay,
Correct, not cold, nor uncontrolled though free,
But proof to all the lures that round us play.[6]

A lover of literature, poet, lawyer and judge, friend to John Henry Newman and Gerard Manley Hopkins, O'Hagan was described in the weekly British magazine, the *Spectator*, as 'known to all not only as a most learned and experienced lawyer with a serene temper and a judgement of rare balance, but as a scholar of wide and liberal culture, a man beloved and respected by all who knew him'.[7]

In the final quarter of his life, O'Hagan was closely associated with the scholars and poets who circulated around the Jesuit, Matthew Russell. He was a frequent contributor to Russell's publication, the *Irish Monthly*, and was, in Russell's view, the best man he had ever known, a virtual Irish Thomas More.

This book is offered in the hope that his memory and achievements will be recovered for posterity. It is written in two parts, in recognition of the change that took place in O'Hagan's life from the end of the 1850s.

6   Cit. Matthew Russell, 'Poets I have known', in *Irish Monthly*, February 1903, pp. 68–9.
7   Cit. M. Russell, in *Irish Monthly*, August 1887, p. 472.

Part 1 (1822–55):
Early Years, Young Irelander, Lawyer

Chapter 1

From Newry to Dublin

Growing up in Newry

John O'Hagan was born in Newry, County Down, on 19 March 1822, the second son of John Arthur O'Hagan, a wool merchant and town commissioner, and Mary Anne (née Cavanagh) from County Armagh. John Arthur O'Hagan was a leader of the Catholic party in Newry and a committed follower of Daniel O'Connell in the drive for Catholic Emancipation.[8]

With the growing pressure for emancipation that was brought about by O'Connell's monster meetings, the first years of John's life were years of determination and excitement for Irish Catholics. The intensity of public feeling was such that the government in Westminster, fearful of revolution, finally passed the Act of Catholic Emancipation in 1829. After that, O'Connell, a hero in the eyes of Catholics, became known to them as 'the Liberator'. While a number of liberal Protestants were supportive of Catholic Emancipation, as John would have learned from his father and from visitors to the house, he would also have known that most Protestants, fearful of the growing freedom and power of Catholics, viewed O'Connell with a mixture of awe and hatred.

John was friendly with a number of Protestant boys in his neighbourhood.[9] Political and religious differences did not enter into their relationships, except for one period each year in mid-summer. During the days leading up to the twelfth of July, Protestants became distant from their Catholic neighbours. On that

---

8 Matthew Russell, 'Judge O'Hagan, Some Notes on his Life and Letters', in *Irish Monthly*, August 1912, pp. 419–23.
9 Among them, John Kells Ingram (1823–1907), remembered for the celebrated ballad he wrote in his twenties, 'Who Fears to Speak of Ninety-Eight?' He remained a lifelong friend of John O'Hagan. 'Ninety-Eight' is a reference to the 1898 insurrection of the United Irishmen, which was crushed by the government.

date, in celebration of a battle fought near the River Boyne in County Meath in 1690, Protestant men put on orange sashes and marched in triumphant procession through the towns and villages of Ulster. These marches frequently ended with speeches denouncing Catholics and insulting the pope.

The Battle of the Boyne had been fought between the Protestant claimant to the throne, William of Orange, and the actual king, James II, who was a Catholic. The battle was won by William, who subsequently won the war in Ireland. The victory of the Protestant forces at the Boyne had significance for both Catholics and Protestants in Ireland. With the support of the English government, the Irish parliament, itself a Protestant body, passed and enforced draconian laws to prohibit the Catholic majority in Ireland ever endangering the Protestant ascendancy. Penal laws were enacted that confiscated the lands of Catholics, deprived them of teachers and education and exiled their bishops. This last measure was enacted in the hope that, without the presence of bishops to ordain new priests, Catholicism would fade away.

Following these measures Catholics, in effect, had no rights under the law. The laws were vigorously and rigorously enforced for the first thirty years of the eighteenth century, but their application began to be notably relaxed from the 1750s. In the second half of that century, Catholics began to agitate for their rights – social, political and religious – to be respected. This reached a high point with Catholic Emancipation in 1829.

It is not clear how much of this background history was absorbed or understood by the young O'Hagan. He was a clever boy, however, and close to his father, who was well-educated and politically active. John senior encouraged his son's literary interests, and even set about working up his own knowledge of Latin in order to help his son with Caesar's Commentaries.[10] Young John began his formal education at the age of eight, when he started to attend a school run by a Dr Henderson.[11]

---

10 Matthew Russell, 'Poets I have known, No. 2, John O'Hagan, Lyrics and Unpublished Letters', in *Irish Monthly*, February 1903, p. 62.
11 *Idem*, pp. 62–3.

From Newry to Dublin

In 1833, when John was eleven years old, his father died. It was a pivotal experience in the young boy's life. Shortly afterwards, he was sent to Dublin to stay with relatives and to attend a new school run by the Jesuits in Hardwicke Street, while his mother remained in Newry for some time to deal with business matters. While no record has survived of the boy's relatives in Dublin, they and some of the Jesuits appear to have been a source of strength and comfort to him as he dealt with the loss of his father, the absence of his mother and the strangeness of his new home.

Having to deal psychologically and spiritually with his father's death had a deepening effect on John, as is suggested by comments made subsequently about the maturity he showed among his contemporaries, and the empathy he manifested for others when they faced difficulties and suffering.[12] That he found help and understanding from his Jesuit teachers is indicated by the observation of a friend that he 'never wavered in his affectionate loyalty to his early teachers at Hardwicke Street'.[13]

12 Gavan Duffy, *Young Ireland: A Fragment of Irish History* , op. cit., p.133.
13 Matthew Russell, 'Judge O'Hagan. Some Notes on his Life and Letters', in *Irish Monthly,* August 1912, p. 426.

CHAPTER 2

Jesuit Education and Trinity College

Hardwicke Street School

In 1817, the Jesuits opened a chapel and community house on a site in Hardwicke Street, Dublin, which had formerly been occupied by the Order of St Clare, popularly known as the Poor Clares. Fifteen years later, with the inauguration of the large Jesuit Church of St Francis Xavier in nearby Gardiner Street, there was no longer any need for the Hardwicke Street chapel, and the superior, Fr Charles Aylmer, converted it into a school. (Nine years later, in 1841, the school would move to Belvedere House in Great Denmark Street, at the top of North Great George's Street, becoming known as Belvedere College.[14])

On 25 August 1832, the *Freeman's Journal* reflected the ethos of the time as it announced the new school in Hardwicke Street, together with its programme and terms. The account commenced with the subheading, 'Under the patronage of His Grace the Most Rev. Dr Murray, the Reverend Gentlemen of St Francis Xavier's Church, Upper Gardiner Street, have opened a Day School, for the literary and moral education of young gentlemen, in the Chapel House, Hardwicke Street, which is now suitably arranged for this purpose.' The account continued:

> The course of Education will comprise, the Latin, Greek, English and French languages, Mathematics, Reading, Writing, Arithmetic, Bookkeeping, History, Geography, etc., etc.,

---

14   For further information on Belvedere College, see John Bowman and Ronan O'Donoghue (eds), *Portraits. Belvedere College, 1832–1982* (Dublin: Gill & Macmillan 1982).

and every branch necessary for a complete Literary and Mercantile Education ... The pupils will be particularly prepared for whatever department in life the parents or guardians may direct ... The usual Classical Course will embrace all that is required for entering Trinity College, or the Roman Catholic College of Maynooth ... Of the system and mode of Education ... particulars may be had ... by application to Rev. Charles Aylmer, the Rev. Robert Haly, or the Rev. John Curtis, at No. 18, Upper Gardiner Street, Dublin.

Further information was provided under the heading 'Terms':

Age of Admission, from seven to fourteen. Pension, three guineas per quarter, to be paid in cash, and in advance ... Hours of attendance from Nine 'till Three o'clock. Music, Dancing, Drawing and Fencing are extra charges – the scholars to provide the necessary books, paper, and all other school requisites, at their own expense ... No scholar will be received or retained, who will not strictly observe the rules and regulations of the school, and conduct himself in every respect as becomes a Christian and a Gentleman. Dublin, August 1st, 1832.

The school in Hardwicke Street was small and unpretentious, chiefly preparatory. Little is known of John's time there after his arrival in 1833. In accordance with the curriculum as outlined above, he would have studied Greek, Latin, English and French, and also some history and geography. He probably received some instruction in philosophy and theology, and initial training in public speaking and debating. Some of the school's students passed on to more notable establishments such as Clongowes Wood College, County Kildare, or Stonyhurst College in England. O'Hagan, however, seems to have continued at the school until he was ready to enter Trinity College, Dublin University.

Trinity College

In 1837, John O'Hagan entered Trinity College, taking his BA degree five years later. It was during those years that he accumulated and absorbed the extensive knowledge and learning for which he became known as a very young man. In particular, he found himself greatly attracted to the Historical Society, which was the focal point for debates and discussion within the college at the time.

Trinity College was undergoing a change in culture during those years. Founded in the sixteenth century as an institution for a Protestant population, it had recently opened its doors in a more liberal direction, and in the years after Emancipation an atmosphere of political excitement was in evidence. The sense of change was almost tangible, as the new Liberal government, supported by O'Connell and his Irish Parliamentary Party, offered the hope of parliamentary reform. Among young educated Catholics a new confidence was emerging, combined with a desire to improve the conditions and prospects of their people. Some young Protestants, too, found in themselves a sense of pride in being Irish, and were also hoping for change. Such feelings found ready expression in Trinity's Historical Society.

A central figure was Thomas Davis (1814–1845), an unassuming young man of great ability and rare charm who unashamedly asserted his pride in being Irish. Born to a Protestant family in Mallow, County Cork, he aimed, politically and socially, 'at uniting all classes and creeds in a patriotic effort to advance national interests, and to raise the whole intellectual, social and moral standard of the Irish people, which had been lowered by centuries of oppression'.[15] Those who followed him in support of such views became known as Young Irelanders, and among them was O'Hagan, who quickly came to admire and, indeed, revere Davis. As a regular participant at Trinity's Historical Society, he became an ardent nationalist following a paper given by John Blake Dillon at a meeting in 1841.[16]

That same year, Dillon and Davis joined the Repeal Association, a mass movement founded by O'Connell who, since his alliance with the Liberal Party was proving less beneficial to Ireland than he had expected, was now seeking a home rule form of government. The aim of the Association was the repeal of the parliamentary union between Great Britain and Ireland and the restoration of an Irish

---

15 T. F. O'Sullivan, 'Thomas Osborne Davis, the Guiding Spirit of *The Nation*', in *The Young Irelanders* (Tralee: The Kerryman Ltd., 1944), pp. 28–9.
16 Sinéad Sturgeon and James Quinn, 'O'Hagan, John', in *Dictionary of Irish Biography* (Cambridge: Cambridge University Press, 2009, 2018).

parliament.[17]

O'Hagan's involvement with the Historical Society and with The National cause proved to be the start of a significant phase in his life. He became an active member of the Young Ireland movement, and was appointed Auditor of the Historical Society for 1842–43. His abilities made an impact on his contemporaries, as testified by the remarks of Gavan Duffy already quoted in the Introduction to this work. His significance, however, has been largely obscured by the attention given to other activists who, unlike O'Hagan, became involved in violent revolution for Irish independence.

O'Hagan had an attractive range of gifts: an impressive intellect, a spontaneous sense of fun, a feeling for words, an empathy for people and a maturity beyond his years, all joined to an essential modesty and absence of self-regard. Among those attracted by his personality was Gavan Duffy, six years his senior and already an active politician and seasoned journalist. He thought so highly of the young O'Hagan's abilities and judgement that he invited him to become one of the select inner circle who produced the weekly newspaper, *The Nation*. Shortly afterwards, Duffy chose O'Hagan to be a companion on his tours of Munster (1844) and Ulster (1845).

The Nation

Named after a Paris journal of that title, *The Nation* was founded in 1842 by Duffy, Davis and Dillon. The first number appeared on 15 October, and it had an almost immediate success. 'Within a few weeks the paper, which combined news, literary criticism, poetry and social and political commentary, was being read all over the country. Those who could not afford 6d to buy it, borrowed it, or read it in the Repeal reading rooms.'[18] Popular verse from the core writers was a common feature from the start.

As an efficient editor, Duffy sought to foster an atmosphere of 'intimate companionship' among the contributors to the paper. For the inner circle, 'Saturday night was planning night', as Duffy recollect-

17 T. F. O'Sullivan, op. cit., loc. cit., p. 28.
18 Laurence McCaffrey, *The Irish Question* (Lexington, KY: University of Kentucky Press, 1968), pp. 41–2, cit. Terrance J. LaRocca, *'The Irish Career of Charles Gavan Duffy, 1840–1855'*, Dissertation, Loyola University Chicago.

ed. 'The inner group of five – Duffy, Davis, Dillon, Pigot, and John O'Hagan, and some others – met by arrangement in one another's homes from tea time to supper time, and into the early hours of the morning literary and political projects were debated and decisions reached as to what was to be written and by whom.'[19] High standards were expected, the writers leaving themselves open to frank criticism during the meetings, and subsequently in correspondence with each other.

This was a valuable formative experience for young writers like O'Hagan and Pigot. As the leader among the writers, Davis helped with the editing, thus enabling Duffy to devote more time to the management side of the paper, in which he was highly competent.[20] William Lecky, the most notable Irish historian of the century,[21] in his *Leaders of Public Opinion in Ireland*, was to observe that 'seldom had a journal exhibited a more splendid combination of eloquence, poetry and reasoning than did *The Nation* under Gavan Duffy's editorship'.[22]

While in Trinity, O'Hagan became a lifelong friend of John Pigot, who was around his own age. He also fitted easily into the company of men like Gavan Duffy who were often older and more experienced than himself. In particular, together with most of his close colleagues in Young Ireland, he had a profound regard for Davis as a deep thinker, a fine scholar, and an unselfish and patriotic man.[23] For his part, O'Hagan also earned the esteem of his colleagues by his clear thinking, his facility with words and the sense of rhyme and rhythm in his poetry. All of these would be put to good use in the pages of *The Nation*.

19 Gavan Duffy, *My Life in Two Hemispheres*, (London: T. fisher Unwin, 1898), pp. 77–9, cit. LaRocca, dissertation cit., p. 14.
20 LaRocca, *idem*, p. 15.
21 William Edward Hartpole Lecky (1838–1903) was a historian and prolific author. His acclaimed works include: *Leaders of Public Opinion in Ireland* (1861); *A History of the Rise and Influence of Rationalism in Europe* (2 vols. 1865); *A History of European Morals from Augustus to Charlemagne* (2 vols, 1869); and – his major work, in eight volumes – *England During the Eighteenth Century* (1878–1890). Formerly a moderate Liberal, in 1895 he was elected to parliament as a Unionist member for Dublin University.
22 William Edward Hartpole Lecky, *Leaders of Public Opinion in Ireland* (London: Longmans Green and Company, 1861), (1903 ed.), vol. 2, p. 283.
23 T. F. O'Sullivan, op. cit., p. 28.

Chapter 3

Writer for The Nation

First Contribution

While most of the writers in *The Nation* wrote under pseudonyms, O'Hagan's first contribution, which appeared on 3 December 1842, was published anonymously. The poem, first entitled 'Aid Yourselves', later became celebrated as 'Ourselves Alone',[24] reflected the demand for independence widely held by members of the Repeal Association. It also reflected the belief that, since the government could not be trusted, independence could only be achieved by the people's own efforts. It caused something of a stir at the time. Two of its verses suffice to convey the 'manliness and strength and maturity wonderful for a youth' that Gavan Duffy found in O'Hagan's poetry.[25]

The work that should today be wrought
Defer not till tomorrow;
The help that should within be sought,
          Scorn from without to borrow.
     Old maxims these yet stout and true –
They speak in trumpet tone:
To do at once what is to do
 And trust ourselves alone.

Too long our Irish hearts were schooled
In patient hope to bide,
By dreams of English justice fooled
And English tongues that lied;
That hour of weak delusion's past –
The empty dream has flown:

---

24 Letter of Davis to O'Hagan, 19 November 1844. In Matthew Russell, 'Poets I have Known, No. 2, John O'Hagan', in *Irish Monthly*, February 1903, p. 66.
25 Cit. M. Russell, *idem*, p. 67.

Our hope and strength, we find at last,
Is in ourselves alone.

This poem later appeared in other poetic selections.[26]

When reprinting O'Hagan's poems in *The Spirit of The Nation*,[27] Davis, without consulting O'Hagan, chose 'Slieve Gullion' or, in Irish, 'Sliabh Cuilin', as a pseudonym for him. When the young man remonstrated good-humouredly at this choice, Davis replied, 'Why not? A fine big mountain in the North.' The name stuck.

Further Poems and Ballads

Another much-quoted poem by O'Hagan, which appeared on 26 August 1843, was entitled 'Paddies Evermore'. While striking a more rollicking note than 'Ourselves Alone', it was a ballad of similar assertiveness:

The hour is passed to fawn or crouch
    As suppliants for our rights;
Let word and deed unshrinking vouch
    The banded millions' might:
        Let them who scorn the fountain rill
Now dread the torrent's roar,
    And hear our echoed chorus still:
        We're Paddies evermore.

The above contributions were almost muted compared to the trenchant, unrelenting tone of 'The Union', first published on 22 April 1843. This poem would become the best known of O'Hagan's poems of this period, particularly because of its stirring and scathing opening verse, which became one of the standard recitations of nationalist Ireland. Reflecting the drive for the Repeal of the Union of Ireland with Great Britain, it expressed the conviction that the Irish

26   These include: John Cooke, ed., *The Dublin Book of Irish Verse 1728–1909* (Dublin: Hodges, 1909); Justin MacCarthy (General Ed.), *Irish Literature* (Seattle, WA: Washington University Press, 1904).

27   *The Spirit of The Nation* was an anthology of ballads and poems reprinted from *The Nation*. It was issued in two parts in 1843 and frequently reprinted thereafter.

parliament had been subsumed into the parliament of Westminster by means of deceit and corruption, including the promise of emancipation made to the Catholic bishops if they supported the union. The major villains in O'Hagan's treatment were Prime Minister William Pitt, and Chief Secretary Lord Castlereagh.

> How did they pass the Union?
> By perjury and fraud;
> > By slaves who sold their land for gold
> > > As Judas sold his God;
> By all the savage acts that yet
> Have followed England's track –
> The pitchcap and the bayonet,
> The gibbet and the rack.
> > And thus was passed the Union
> > > By Pitt and Castlereagh;
> Could Satan send for such an end
> > More worthy tools than they?

O'Hagan could also strike a gentler, but still patriotic, tone, as is clear from the first verse of the poem entitled 'Dear Land':

> When comes the day all hearts to weigh
> If staunch they be, or vile,
> Shall we forget the sacred debt
> We owe our mother isle?
> My native heath is brown beneath,
> My native waters blue;
> But crimson red o'er both shall spread
> Ere I am false to you,
> Dear land,
> Ere I am false to you.

Justin McCarthy, editor of *Irish Literature*,[28] included 'Dear Land' as well as 'Ourselves Alone' in his publication, and both also ap-

28 Op. cit.

peared in *The Spirit of The Nation*.[29] On a more personal note, Gavan Duffy is said to have had a particular regard for 'Dear Land', and is reported to have recited the opening lines on his deathbed.

O'Hagan sometimes wrote a different kind of verse under another pseudonym, 'Caroline Wilhelmina Amelia'. The first lines of 'Missing at Sea' are a good example of this style of writing:

Alone and pacing to and fro
Or peering on the waves below,
Rise fast within me, as I muse
Regrets, resolves, and sad adieus.

The occasion of this poem was not, as might be assumed, O'Hagan's departure for London in October 1845. In fact, it was written to commemorate a very different occasion: the first anniversary of Thomas Davis's death on 16 September 1845, aged thirty. The passing of his hero shocked O'Hagan deeply, and caused him – as well as all those who knew and admired Davis – great anguish. His death would also be a blow to the future of *The Nation*.

The poetry published in *The Nation* must be viewed in the context of its time. W. B. Yeats, who had been introduced to the poems of Thomas Davis by the old Fenian, John O'Leary, conceded that, while they may not have been very good poetry, they moved him because they 'spoke, or tried to speak, out of the people to the people; behind them stretched the generations'.[30] It is an observation that might be applied to a number of *The Nation's* poets, including O'Hagan. Despite the limits of the genre, Matthew Russell, long-time editor of the *Irish Monthly* and O'Hagan's close friend, had a high estimation of O'Hagan's potential as a poet. Some of this would be realised in O'Hagan's poetic work in later years.

29 T. F. O'Sullivan, op. cit., p. 308.
30 T. W. Hayek, 'The Genealogy of Irish Modernism: the case of W.B. Yeats', in Stewart J. Brown and David W. Miller (eds), *Piety and Power in Ireland, 1760–1960: Essays in Honour of Emmet Larkin* (Belfast: Institute of Irish Studies, the Queen's University, 2000), p. 245. John O'Leary (1830–1907) was a member of the Irish Republican Brotherhood, known as the Fenians, who organised an unsuccessful revolution in Ireland in 1867.

Moving On

In 1843, the year in which he wrote many of his poems for *The Nation*, O'Hagan decided, despite his attraction to literature, to opt for a career in law. He was accepted for Lincoln's Inn in London, where he would find himself studying alongside his friend from Trinity, John Pigot. Before that, however, he would embark on a tour of south Leinster and Munster with Gavan Duffy and another friend, Denis Florence MacCarthy.[31]

Thomas Davis, Young Irelander

All three kept diaries of their tour, but O'Hagan's was longer and more detailed than the others, since he planned to submit it for publication to the *Irish Monthly*. When it was published, under the title 'Leinster and Munster in the Summer of 1844', O'Hagan used a version of his pseudonym from *The Nation*, 'Sliabh Gullian', and in the text sometimes referred to Duffy as 'the Black Northerner', and MacCarthy as 'Desmond'. Duffy and O'Hagan, both northerners, had never been further south than Dublin, and MacCarthy, though his name was that of a distinguished Munster family, seems at this point to have spent his entire life in Dublin. Understandably, then, there was a sense of adventure about their journey, as will become apparent in the next chapter.

31 Denis Florence MacCarthy (1817–1882) was born in Dublin. He was a poet, editor and translator. He edited *Poets and Dramatists of Ireland* in 1846 and, around the same time, *The Book of Irish Ballads*. In 1850 he produced his *Ballads, Poems and Lyrics*. He earned a permanent place in English letters with his translation and interpretation of the works of Pedro Calderón de la Barca. The first volume, containing six plays, appeared in 1853, and others followed in 1861, 1867, 1870 and 1873. He lived at Killiney, County Dublin, until 1864, when he went to the Continent for reasons of health, before settling in London. He returned to Ireland months before his death on Good Friday 1882. A tribute to him by his friend John O'Hagan appeared in the *Freeman's Journal* on Easter Monday of that year.

CHAPTER 4

Travels in South Leinster and Munster

Delayed Departure

As they prepared for a quiet holiday touring the countryside and enjoying each other's company, the little group of friends found their plans unexpectedly disrupted. On 30 May 1844, prior to their departure, Daniel O'Connell, his son John (also a Member of Parliament), Thomas Ray (Secretary of the Repeal Association), Charles Gavan Duffy (Editor of *The Nation*) and four others were found guilty 'of conspiring to excite ill-will among the Queen's subjects and to obtain by unlawful methods a change in the government and constitution of the country'.[32] Imprisoned together, the 'Traversers', as they came to be known, spent the time, in Duffy's words, 'in as little unpleasantness as a holiday in a country-house'.[33]

Three months later, when their sentences were overturned, the Traversers' release was greeted enthusiastically with countrywide celebrations, as O'Hagan and his companions would find out on their travels. They would be surprised by the number of people who recognised Duffy and knew of his imprisonment along with O'Connell and the others.

Kilkenny, Wexford and Waterford

O'Hagan's journal was written in a lively, youthful and sometimes humorous spirit. He explained how the three companions set out just after eight o'clock on the morning of 11 September, with Kilkenny as their destination. Travelling in horse-drawn vehicles, they

32   T. F. O'Sullivan, 'Charles Gavan Duffy, editor of *The Nation*', in op.. cit., p. 10.
33   Duffy – Davis, May 1844, Duffy Papers, cit. LaRocca, op. cit. p. 15.

passed the time on the long journey 'reciting and quoting an infinity of poetry'.

The beauty and tidiness of the city of Kilkenny impressed them, but O'Hagan found himself irritated when some gentlemen arrived who wished to talk politics with O'Connell's fellow prisoner. (Subsequently in his account, O'Hagan would playfully refer to Duffy as 'The Martyr' or 'The Repeal Martyr'.) O'Hagan noted that 'Kilkenny county, as far as I saw of it, contains a splendid peasantry – fine men and exceedingly handsome women, and both well dressed. We remarked, too, that there was very little servility, very little "your Honouring" about them. They are kindly to a degree, and at the same time have a free independent manner which it is most inspiring to see.'

From New Ross, County Wexford, the three travellers wished to visit the site of 'the great battle' of 1798, and they were brought to the location by a local man, Martin Doyle, who had himself witnessed the battle. Subsequently, O'Hagan reflected on this visit. He noted that he had seen in 'old Martin Doyle' something he had observed several times before, 'that those who were actors or witnesses in the scenes of '98 have the strongest horror of any appeal to arms at present, and are the warmest supporters of O'Connell's peaceful policy'. He then went on to ask rhetorically, 'Ought not we in our ignorance learn from those who know what civil war is?'

Reflecting further on the political situation, and thinking especially of those Young Irelanders who were impatient with O'Connell and talked of armed rebellion, O'Hagan wrote:

> It is utter folly to say that 'Young Ireland', as a party distinct from O'Connell, has any hold on the minds of the people. *The Nation* has immense circulation as the ablest Repeal organ, but it is O'Connell and the priests who are the bone and marrow of the movement. The 'Tibetism', as Davis calls it, of the people to O'Connell is beyond anything I could have conceived. I saw one woman prostrate herself before Duffy – 'the gentleman that was in prison with Mr O'Connell'.

From New Ross the little group sailed down the Barrow to Waterford, their first taste of the province of Munster. As before, Duffy was recognised and there was a public welcome for the group, prompting

O'Hagan to comment, 'We are living too fast ... getting enveloped by priests and popular huzzas and bonfires and bands for the Repeal Martyr. Endless notoriety.'

In Cappoquin, 'a beautiful little village on the Blackwater river', they found the peace and enjoyment they desired. From there they visited the nearby Trappist monastery of Mount Melleray, where they were greatly impressed by what the monks had accomplished on the barren mountainside. Before leaving Cappoquin, they visited the national primary school, where O'Hagan remarked on 'the amount of knowledge and intelligence of the children in these schools'.

Cork City and County

O'Hagan had high expectations of Cork city, 'the southern Athens on the banks of the "silvery Lee"'. His hopes were partly based on a popular poem by 'Father Prout' extolling the bells of Shandon Church, situated on 'the pleasant waters of the River Lee'.[34] Instead of the anticipated romantic setting, however, O'Hagan found that 'Shandon Church stands in the very middle of Cork; its excessively ugly steeple rising above a crowd of uglier house tops.' He went on dismissively that 'you might as well talk of the pleasant waters of the Liffey at Carlisle Bridge as of the Lee beside Shandon Church'.

If the city itself proved disappointing, O'Hagan recalled with pleasure the meeting the three travellers had with the Capuchin priest, Fr Theobald Mathew. Known throughout Ireland for his campaign to promote temperance, he invited the visitors to dine with him at his house, where he spoke at length with them.

A friend of Fr Mathew's brought the three travellers to Blarney, north-west of the city, and then to Cove (later Queenstown, now Cobh), some miles to the east. When they reached Blarney, O'Hagan and MacCarthy, with youthful elan, made straight for the castle and raced up the steps to kiss the Blarney Stone. Afterwards they amused each other with extravagant language as an exercise in 'blarney'. Duffy, meanwhile, lingered in the groves of Blarney, made famous by Richard Alfred Milliken's ballad of that name. Later they

---

34 The reference is to the song 'The Bells of Shandon', written by Father Prout (pseudonym of Francis Sylvester Mahony, 1806–1866), in which these lines are repeated: 'The bells of Shandon / Sound far more grand on / The pleasant waters of the River Lee'.

took the steamer to Cove, which impressed them with its magnificent harbour and raised their estimation of Cork, 'or more properly the outlets of Cork'.

The next morning, 22 September, at breakfast in Fr Mathew's house, they were introduced to drisheen, a local Cork dish 'made of something like black puddings', and 'after breakfast went to Mass in Fr Mathew's chapel'. Subsequently, on a visit with him to the Ursuline convent in a covered car, an unexpected incident left O'Hagan 'more and more struck with Fr Mathew's thorough goodness and kindness of heart'. They 'passed a row of orphan boys belonging to some institution. He stopped the car and sent 2 shillings to the usher to buy apples for the boys.' Following this incident, Fr Mathew made a comment that greatly impressed O'Hagan. The priest remarked 'that he never knew boys brought up in these institutions to turn out well, because they were devoid of all natural ties'. They cared for nobody and nobody cared for them, he said, 'whereas, he knew several instances where orphan infants had been sent out to nurse and their foster mothers grew so fond of them that they said they would die rather than part with them … Those children, being treated with kindness and affection, grew up good members of society.'

That evening they were invited once again to dinner in Fr Mathew's house, where there was a party of about a dozen people. After the meal, 'our host brought in a whole file of newspapers and pitched them on the table for the entertainment of the guests'. At this point, O'Hagan tells of an embarrassing incident which points to a youthful impulsiveness in him. 'I read some verse out of a Connacht paper to excite the laughter of the company. When I came to the end, I discovered to my horror that they were copies from the *Cork Examiner*. Near fainting at the thought that they might have been written by someone present, I found they were the production of a friend of a gentleman opposite.'

Leaving Cork city behind, they headed west on the long journey to Glengarriff, arriving there during the night. Glengarriff lived up to their expectations, as is clear from O'Hagan's description of their time there. 'We wandered about the shores of the sweet little bay of Glengariff without care, aim or guide … We laid ourselves down upon green spots, looking down on the water, and read poetry to one another. Walked again in the evening; delicious twilight and full moon upon the bay.'

Next day, O'Hagan persuaded MacCarthy to join him on an expedition to climb Hungry Hill, a mountain of some 685 metres further west near Adrigool. To get there, they rowed west from Glengariff into Bantry Bay, where O'Hagan 'thought of the French and poor Wolfe Tone'.[35] At Adrigool they prepared for the ascent – 'no joke of an undertaking' – with the help of a local guide. They were looking forward to seeing the reputedly fine view from the summit and, on arrival, found that the splendid sight well repaid the effort.

By the time they finished their descent, night had fallen, their feet were wet, and they were hungry. Despite the inconvenience, however, O'Hagan wrote in lyrical fashion about their journey home: 'I never remember a lovelier night. It was full moon without a cloud, and the waters so still that the moon's image was unbroken except by the fall of the oars. One of the boatmen … under the influence of the moon, sang love ditties without end'. Arriving back in Glengariff at half-past ten, they found that Duffy, who was beginning to be a little uneasy about them, had prepared a good fire in the room. Then: 'meat and tea, poetry, and to bed'.

'The Kingdom of Kerry'

Leaving County Cork behind, the three visitors headed for Kenmare, in neighbouring County Kerry. The winding road threaded its way through a mountainous district, at one point entering 'a tunnel cut in the solid rock in the centre of which is the boundary between Cork and Kerry'. There they gave three cheers on entering the renowned 'Kingdom of Kerry'.

O'Hagan began his account of their time in Kerry with their visit to Killarney and its lakes. It was 'the first place I have ever seen which has surpassed the idea I had formed of it … We were all through the

---

35 Theobald Wolfe Tone (1763–1798) was a leading Irish revolutionary figure and one of the founders of the United Irishmen. He went to France to seek military aid, and in 1796 was part of a French force of forty-three ships and some 14,450 men which arrived in Bantry Bay. Unable to land because of weather conditions, they returned to France. Two years later, in a further expedition, Tone was captured and is said to have taken his own life in prison.

Middle and Lower Lakes, and landed on the lovely islands of Ross, Innisfallen, and Dinis.' A bugler who accompanied them 'awoke the echoes in several places'.

On Monday, 30 September, O'Hagan recorded that they had gone on the previous day 'to the great Gap of Dunloe, having first heard Mass in Killarney chapel'. On their way to the Gap, they met members of a congregation coming from a country chapel. Noting that they were 'well dressed and good-looking', O'Hagan reflected on his impressions to date. He recalled that, had he been asked before his travels where he expected to find the best-off people, he would have said County Cork. In fact, he now recorded, they had seen 'more marks of wretchedness in the County Cork than through all the rest of their route'. He acknowledged, however, that they had travelled 'through the poorest part of it'.

The next evening, in Kenmare, 'the good people ... found that they had caught a martyr. Two large tar-barrels burned in front of the hotel. A large circle [was] made round the fire. There was dancing and music.' O'Hagan and MacCarthy enjoyed the scene, and then sat on 'in the long room after Duffy went to bed, until at length they followed his example'.

During this time, O'Hagan recorded an incident which reflected badly on both MacCarthy and himself, revealing quite callow behaviour in these young men who were otherwise mature and sensitive. A deputation from Killarney came to visit Duffy, speaking 'in what English slanderers call the "ultra-Irish style", commencing with, "Is it true, can it be possible that you, you so late the inmate of a penitentiary ... "'. O'Hagan went on to describe the reaction of the two young travellers: 'Desmond and I turned our faces to the fire in torture to suppress our laughter ... [it] finished without a burst, though our contortions were perceived.' When the deputation had departed, Duffy berated them for their levity, saying that they 'should look to the real earnestness and good intentions of the people, not the manner of its expression'. Accepting the admonition, they 'admitted this to be true'.

In Kenmare, the travellers were awaiting an opportunity to visit Daniel O'Connell's home in Derrynane, which was the main objec-

Daniel O'Connell's home at Derrynane.

tive of their visit to Kerry. Once they received word that O'Connell was in residence, they set out on the tortuous journey, noting 'in general the extreme wildness of the country and the wretchedness of the inhabitants'. As they drew nearer to Derrynane, however, they noticed a change, 'as if we were coming into the territory of some old chieftain. Saw scouts and outposts in the shape of postboys and red-coated huntsmen'. Then: 'Arrived at last.'

Sojourn in Derrynane

O'Hagan continued with his first impressions: 'No picture I ever saw gives at all a correct idea of the house, which is a very irregular mansion, built at various periods, a good deal of it weather slated.' Since 'his father at that moment was in the bath', they 'were received most cordially by John O'Connell', the great man's son. O'Hagan was overjoyed to find that John Pigot and his brother David were also staying in the house. Having been introduced to John's wife and to a Miss Staunton in the drawing room, the visitors went to their bedrooms to dress. They then returned to the drawing room, where they sat talking until dinner time. It was in the dining room that, for the first time since their arrival, they met O'Connell, who gave them a 'hearty welcome'.

O'Hagan recalled that 'the dinner was very profuse', with 'wines of numberless species', but as he wrote he could not recollect anything remarkable about the conversation. They later withdrew to the drawing room for tea and some further talk, after which they retired to bed early. O'Connell, it transpired, had plans for them for the next day. He 'had arranged that we were to start early, a hunt before breakfast, and, when two hares were caught and, not before, breakfast on the sod'.

The following morning, O'Hagan rose at seven o'clock, only to find 'the morning looking very inauspicious. Walked out with Duffy to see the unbroken surge rolling from Labrador. It was very grand. The situation of Derrynane is one of the most magnificent I can conceive, just the place to fill one with great thoughts and unbounded love of freedom. Walked back to the house and found the hunt was abandoned.'

The weather did not improve during the day. 'After breakfast, rain, rain. Our friend the weather, who had treated us in so considerate a manner, [was] beginning to desert us ... Ran out in a fair blink with Duffy, MacCarthy and the Pigots to the seashore. The sand of the finest description, just the sort of strand ladies delight to bathe in. Caught by a shower. Ran back and changed our clothes.'

They ventured out 'twice more during the remainder of this showery day – once when O'Connell took them through his garden and kennel, the latter considered very fine; even I, who, Lord knows, have small interest in hunting matters, was struck by the fine appearance of the dogs as dogs'. O'Hagan then went on to comment on a striking exchange between O'Connell and his huntsman:

Our 'Cur-a-muck' (I suppose it is the same name as Cormac) ... delights in speaking boldly, and even, as it seems to me, impertinently, to his master, who indulges him in it. Reminded me of Napoleon using greater freedom with his privates than with his marshals. (Mem. – O'Connell speaks chiefly in Irish to his outdoor servants).

Meanwhile, there was 'a new invasion of visitors. The family of Mr Primrose, O'Connell's agent, three old maids'. Also visiting were a Fr

Rooney of Westland Row, Dublin, a Fr Jerry O'Sullivan, an old major ('at least he is called major by everyone') who acted as O'Connell's master of the hounds, and a Dr O'Connor, 'a queer genius'.

That evening at dinner, the three representatives of *The Nation* were much taken by O'Connell's conversation. 'We were quite surprised to find his knowledge so varied, and such intimacy with books. Talk about Shelley, who made a speech at a Catholic meeting in Dublin in 1812, but which O'Connell did not remember. He spoke in praise of Goethe's Faust.'

At this point, O'Hagan interrupted his narrative and did not return to it. Instead, following a reminder by MacCarthy, he went back to the conversation they had had with O'Connell after dinner on the previous night, the night of their arrival. On that occasion, wrote O'Hagan, O'Connell 'spoke of his keeping guard as a yeoman in Emmet's insurrection in 1803. He also said he was a yeoman in '98 and, nevertheless, was a United Irishman. Tasked by John Pigot rather strictly as to his reconciliation of the apparently inconsistent offices, he said that after the insurrection of '98 the popular party was so completely crushed that the only chance of doing any good for the people was by affecting ultra-loyalty. O'Hagan was not impressed, but Duffy remarked to him afterwards 'that we, with our freeborn notions, can have but little idea of the position of men in those days of terror and oppression'.

After dinner on their second evening, there was tea in the drawing room. A couple of harpers provided music, and in no time they were dancing 'quadrilles and Sir Roger de Coverley with great vigour. Happened, as usual, that very few of us knew it, so we had even more than the ordinary amount of confusion. [There were] jigs, too, by John O'Connell, Dr O'Connor and the Misses Primrose.' O'Hagan then added, 'O'Connell, himself, always retires very early.'

O'Hagan provided a full account of their third day in Derrynane:
On Friday [we were] up at 8 o'clock, just in time for Mass. The morning wet again, confound it! Reading newspapers after breakfast. It cleared up at length, and we went out to hunt. All on foot except Duffy and Miss Staunton, who followed up on pony-back. We saw the hunt from an old Irish rath, the

site of the residence of a chief.

We had a good view of the hunt. O'Connell always hunts with beagles. He has a detestation of greyhounds. I was sickened at seeing the hare brought back all torn and mangled. Rain came on, so Duffy and I ran home, he leaving his pony to David Pigot to escort Miss Staunton home. [We] changed our clothes and sat in the library till dinner.

O'Connell came in, and we had a good deal of interesting conversation. He said that when he was a boy, tea, coffee, brandy, wines, etc. were brought direct from France to that part of the country, revenue police being unknown. He remembered distinctly the first time a bottle of whiskey was seen in Kerry. He spoke also of his having seen, when he was a child of three years old, three men who had made their escape from Paul Jones.[36]

At dinner that evening there was 'an abundance of fish, all caught by John O'Connell the day before. They live quite independently of the world in Derrynane. They kill their own meat, catch their own fish, bake their own bread, have their own butter, honey etc. [There was] gaggery at dinner about David Pigot and Miss Staunton, who had been seen galloping off in the direction of the chapel, accompanied by the priest.'

Afterwards in the drawing-room, we 'danced Sir Roger again with tenfold vigour. John O'Connell dancing in an insane manner … He [John O'Connell] strikes me, as indeed he always did, as being kindly, good-humoured, hospitable, and playful to a degree. His father also was as kind to us as he could possibly be.'

At this point, O'Hagan's printed account concludes abruptly with the words, 'The End'.

Reflecting on the Tour

From reading O'Hagan's account of their travels, it appears that the three friends usually stayed in hotels in the larger towns, from which they ventured beyond the main streets to view monuments, historic

---

36 Paul Jones (1747–1792) was an American naval commander, viewed by Britain as a pirate.

ruins and places of scenic beauty. They were frequently treated as celebrities because of Duffy's time in prison with O'Connell, and also his own role as editor of *The Nation*. O'Hagan and MacCarthy clearly enjoyed high spirits along the way, and their rather carefree joie de vivre and spontaneity occasionally landed them, and especially O'Hagan, in embarrassing situations. Duffy comes across as the senior, more experienced, figure, but he too joined with his companions in reading and reciting poetry.

Despite his youthful high spirits, O'Hagan showed himself to be a perceptive observer and commentator. He was clearly impressed by the dignity of the people in County Kilkenny, just as he was disturbed by the wretched social conditions he observed in Cork and Kerry. In New Ross, reflecting on his meeting with Martin Doyle and others who had first-hand knowledge of the 1798 revolution, O'Hagan made clear his opposition to any future revolution and his commitment to peaceful activity. Still in New Ross, he reflected on the towering stature of O'Connell, and his importance, and that of the priests, to the Young Ireland Movement as its 'bone and marrow'. These last two observations reflect a concern O'Hagan was harbouring at the time about emerging trends in Young Ireland.

A sense of freshness, even wonder, emerges from parts of O'Hagan's diary, suggesting how much the tour enhanced his knowledge of his country and its people. Commenting on their visits to Kilkenny, Wexford, Waterford, Cork and Kerry, he noted in particular some special people they met – Fr Mathew, Daniel O'Connell and his son John – and marvelled at the beautiful scenery. He noted the benefits to children of the newly established national schools, and remarked on the friendliness of the people and their devotion to O'Connell. The visit to Derrynane was the anticipated goal of their journey, and their informal, familial reception there, recorded at some length, suggests that it was indeed the highlight of their tour. All the more surprising, then, is the abrupt termination of O'Hagan's narrative, while they were still enjoying O'Connell's hospitality in Derrynane.

CHAPTER 5

Growing Disagreements and Further Travels

Emerging Differences

O'Hagan made the abrupt, final entry in his travel journal on 4 October 1844. It coincided with an event that took place at a meeting of the Repeal Association, reflecting the differences that were emerging between O'Connell and the leaders of Young Ireland. A letter from O'Connell was read at the meeting, indicating his intention to abandon support for Repeal in favour of federation.[37] This was an unwelcome turn of events for the Young Irelanders. In *The Nation*, Duffy hurriedly published an open letter critical of federalism. In it he insisted that there must be no surrender of *The National* demand for the restoration of an independent Irish parliament, which had been the aim of the Repeal Association from the start. After a short time, O'Connell returned to his former position.[38]

A further area of disagreement with O'Connell, one which affected O'Hagan more immediately, concerned the issue of non-denominational university education. Davis, Duffy, O'Hagan and most of the Young Ireland party favoured such education as an aid towards uniting the members of different denominations in Ireland. It was also, they believed, the form of third-level education most likely to win the approval of the Liberal government in Westminster. The proposal, first put forward by Sir Thomas Wyse (MP for Waterford, 1835–47), evoked a hostile reaction from O'Connell, however, who spoke of the proposed institutions as 'the Godless colleges'. Many of

---

37 Federation envisaged an Irish parliament that would be confined to domestic affairs, with continuing Irish representation at Westminster.
38 T. F. O'Sullivan, *The Young Irelanders* (Tralee: The Kerryman, 1944), p. 12. Before long, strong opposition to the idea of federation prompted O'Connell to return to advocating Repeal and, indeed, to open criticism of federation.

Cardinal Paul Cullen

the Catholic clergy sided with him, including a number of bishops led by Archbishops Paul Cullen of Armagh and John McHale of Tuam.[39]

Lucas's Warning

The proposed university system posed a threat to the Repeal Movement and to the unity of those seeking reform, as O'Hagan was to read in a letter written by Frederick Lucas on 27 November 1844. Lucas (1812–1855) was an English journalist and founder of the Catholic newspaper, *The Tablet*. O'Hagan greatly admired him and, indeed, at one stage considered embarking on a career as a Catholic journalist in the mode of Lucas. It appears that O'Hagan had earlier contacted Lucas, who, like so many others, felt himself drawn to the personality and enthusiasm of the young O'Hagan. They later became friends.

Aware of how close O'Hagan and Duffy were, Lucas wrote to O'Hagan in the hope that he might persuade Duffy and *The Nation* to cease supporting the non-denominational colleges. About the proposed university bill, he was quite definite: 'That measure – except by a miracle – will divide clergy and laity, and (with other things) in all human probability will break up the present union of liberal Irishmen. I begin to despair of Repeal, and I know rather more than I choose (or, indeed, am at liberty) to write.' Lucas then went on to elaborate further:

> I know from several quarters that the clergy are bent against Wyse's scheme ... One day or other a large portion of the clergy will declare against Wyse, and then, if *The Nation*

---

39 A considerable number of bishops, led by Archbishop Murray of Dublin, were prepared to accept the Queen's Colleges, as they were called, in order to make free university education possible for the Catholic population. They anticipated that changes would take place in time, as had happened in the case of the National System of Education for primary schools.

should happen to be deeply committed to him, the result must be serious. Surely there can be no harm (no degrada tion) in Duffy calling on Dr Miley[40] and talking over this question with him. What liberality or toleration is there in refusing to the Church the guardianship of her own subjects in the way her most enlightened ministers think essential to their safety? I had no intention of writing on this last subject when I began, but my mind, heart, and soul are full of it, and I can neither write nor think of any other.

At the end of the letter, Lucas adds, 'Kind regards to Duffy, to whom a great part of this ought to have been written.'

Rumours and Divisions

Presuming that O'Hagan passed on Lucas's message to Duffy, there is no evidence of its having any immediate effect. Duffy, Davis and O'Hagan remained committed as before to the proposed university system as a potentially unifying force in the country. The rift Lucas feared became apparent when, in 1845, non-denominational Queen's Colleges in Cork, Galway and Belfast were established by Act of Parliament. Davis's prominence in the movement, together with the independent stand taken by *The Nation*, prompted hostility towards him among O'Connell's supporters. In the ensuing heat, some of O'Connell's followers circulated rumours that Davis was a danger-ous intriguer and infidel, and that his friends acquiesced in his dark desires.[41] These rumours had an influence on many of the Catholic clergy, with the result that sales of *The Nation* suffered.

At a meeting of the Repeal Association in Dublin in May 1845, O'Connell publicly accused Davis of being anti-Catholic and op-posed to Repeal, declaring that he, O'Connell, stood for Old Ireland not Young Ireland.[42] Davis was visibly upset by the charges. He de-nied that he was anti-Catholic, protested his admiration for O'Con-

---

40 John Miley (1806–1861) was a priest in Dublin's Pro-Cathedral (1831–49), and later rector of the Irish College in Rome (1849–58). Despite Archbishop Murray's opposition to his priests being involved in politics, he was an openly staunch supporter of O'Connell and Repeal. See J. A. Gaughan, *The Archbishops, Bishops, Priests of the Archdiocese of Dublin in the 19th Century* (Dublin: Kingdom Books, 2013).

41 Duffy – Dillon, May 1845. Duffy Papers, cit. T. J. LaRocca, op. cit., p. 33.

42 See *The Nation*, May 1845, for an account of the meeting of the Repeal Association.

nell, and asserted his support for Repeal by peaceful means. Amity was restored at the end of the meeting, but hurt feelings lingered on one side, while distrust and suspicion continued on the other.[43]

O'Hagan's conviction about the futility of violence, already apparent during his tour of Munster, was now reignited. He knew the depth of popular support for O'Connell and was convinced that Repeal could not be achieved without him. But he was also aware that some members of Young Ireland felt O'Connell to be now too old and no longer effective, and that violent revolution was the way forward. The emerging political tensions concerned O'Hagan greatly. As August approached, however, he was able to look forward to a respite from them, as he planned a tour of Ulster with three of his companions. His account of this tour, entitled 'Ulster in the Summer of 1845', would be published many years later.[44]

Down and Fermanagh

The Ulster enterprise lacked the novelty and sense of adventure experienced in the earlier tour of South Leinster and Munster. All those taking part – Duffy, John Mitchel,[45] John Martin,[46] and O'Hagan himself – were Ulstermen: Duffy came from Monaghan, Mitchel and O'Hagan grew up in Newry, and Martin was a farmer from outside Newry. United by their nationalist convictions, Mitchel and Martin were Presbyterians, Duffy and O'Hagan were Catholics. The venture would lose much of its appeal for O'Hagan when Duffy, quite early in the tour, was obliged to leave them, having received a letter informing him that his wife, Emily, was critically ill.

The memorable part of the tour, before Duffy's departure, included visits to Downpatrick and Enniskillen. In Downpatrick, they visited the cathedral, the reputed site of St Patrick's grave, and the

---

43 T. J. LaRocca, op. cit., pp. 31–2.

44 O'Hagan's report appeared in the *Irish Monthly,* vol. 41, January 1913.

45 John Mitchel (1815–1875) was an Irish nationalist, author of the *Jail Journal,* and a leading writer for *The Nation.* He broke with O'Connell, advocated a social revolutionary policy during the Irish Famine, was arrested and transported to Tasmania. He escaped and made his way to the US, where he became prominent on the pro-slavery side.

46 John Martin (1812–1875) was the son of a Presbyterian clergyman; of independent means, he travelled to the US in 1839 and to continental Europe in 1841. A Young Ireland nationalist, he joined in the secession from O'Connell, and openly advocated revolution and forcible separation from Britain. He was arrested and sent to Tasmania. He returned to Ireland for family reasons in 1858 and lived there until his death.

Protestant graveyard in which Thomas Russell[47] was buried. 'He was hanged', O'Hagan wrote about Russell, 'for a futile attempt to rouse the North to join that maddest and silliest of all insurrections – Emmet's rising in 1803.'[48] They arrived late at Denvir's Hotel, Downpatrick. After dinner, they read aloud Carlyle's *Sartor Resartus* with great enjoyment before going to bed. In the town of Enniskillen, in County Fermanagh, they witnessed a major Orange celebration. 'There were assembled perhaps 20,000 men with upwards of a 100 flags … They marched in great order through the main street of the town and down again, and out to the hill of meeting. Duffy, Mitchel and I walked out with them – poor Martin being very ill.' At the meeting, Mitchel and O'Hagan found a place reasonably near the platform, while Duffy, having met some Orange friends, was invited onto the platform. In the evening there were 'Protestant processions through the town with torches and music', and a noisy 'Protestant dinner in the market-house next door to the hotel'. The overall experience left O'Hagan tired and critical of his Orange fellow countrymen.[49] O'Hagan summed up the speeches on 'the hill of meeting' as follows:

1. Quotations from Scripture - 'Not to walk after the lusts of the flesh' and other quotations.

2. Vague abuse of Prime Minister Peel.

3. The 'vainest of vain bluster about repealing the Emancipation Act etc.'

4. Allusions of the Boyne, Aughrim etc. and to the physical force of the Orangemen. In O'Hagan's view, there was not 'the remotest approach to any practical proposal, nor the shadow of a course laid down'.

47 Thomas Russell (1767–1803) was born in County Cork. He helped to found the United Irishmen movement in Belfast and Dublin, and tried to organise support for Robert Emmet's rising in the north. On Emmet's capture, he travelled to Dublin in the hope of rescuing him, but was himself arrested and sent to Downpatrick Gaol, where he was hanged.
48 Robert Emmet (1778–1803) was a member of an Irish Protestant ascendancy family. He became republican in outlook and led an abortive rebellion in Dublin in 1803. Found guilty of high treason, he was hanged. His speech from the dock inspired generations of Irish patriots in Ireland and America, and his final lines became part of the patriotic heritage: 'When my country takes its place among the nations of the earth, then, and not till then, let my epitaph be written.'
49 On this account of the Enniskillen processions etc., see *Irish Monthly, idem*, May 1913, pp. 289–90.

Visiting Donegal and Derry

On the way to Donegal, O'Hagan commented on the poverty he observed:

> The same appearance of poverty and squalor here as in the South and other parts of Ireland. No wonder – like causes will always produce like results. The Catholics, robbed of the rich lands, and trampled and plundered in every possible way, became an inferior people (in outward things) as well in Donegal as in Kerry.

It was in Donegal town that Duffy received the unhappy message that his wife was critically ill, necessitating his return home. Duffy's absence clearly had a negative impact on O'Hagan, and there is little joy or poetry-reading recorded for the remainder of the group's travels. Instead, he mentions their many expeditions and endless trekking over mountains and moors throughout Donegal. Later, in Rathmelton, before crossing Lough Swilly on their way to Derry, they received a somewhat reassuring letter from Duffy, telling them that 'he had found Mrs Duffy quite as well as he left her'.

On arriving at their hotel in Derry, they washed and then sallied forth 'for a walk round the walls'. They viewed 'the monument raised to Walker and the other heroes of the siege of Derry in 1689',[50] who held the city for King William against a blockade by King James II's forces. To his shame, O'Hagan admitted that he did not ask a single question about the events of the siege. 'Besides my natural carelessness on such points, I was annoyed by two great dampers of interest: toothache and indigestion.' A few sentences later, he brought his account of the tour to a conclusion with the terse entry, 'Went to see the cathedral. Gothic; handsome – but not so handsome as Downpatrick.'

The tour of Ulster was not much of a holiday for O'Hagan, especially after Duffy had left, but he adapted to the changed circumstances and committed himself to the success of the remainder of the tour. Along the way, he noted the poverty of the Catholic population and the cause of their degradation. He got on well with the northern

---

50 Rev. George Walker (1645–1690) was Governor of Derry during the siege of the city, and author of *True Account of the Siege of Londonderry, 1689.*

Protestants, both Presbyterian and Church of Ireland, although he was uncomfortable with and critical of the expressed political and religious views of the Orangemen they met. The overall experience and the change of scene probably helped him as he came face to face with the challenges that lay ahead.

CHAPTER 6

Studies in London and Divisions in Ireland

The Death of Davis

On his return to Dublin and *The Nation* in early September 1845, O'Hagan found the atmosphere somewhat muted. Duffy was active as editor, as before, but he was concerned for his wife, who was seriously ill with consumption. Moreover, Davis was said to be laid up with some ailment or other, and was nowhere in evidence. The absence of his stimulating personality was felt acutely, but it did not prepare Duffy and his colleagues for the calamity that awaited them. On being summoned urgently to Davis's house at 67 Lower Baggot Street on 16 September, Duffy found that his friend had already died; after a week's illness, Davis, at thirty years of age, had succumbed to a bout of scarlet fever.[51] 'It was,' Duffy declared, 'as if the light had suddenly gone out of the sky.'[52]

Duffy, already occupied with *The Nation* and still concerned for his wife's health, now turned his mind to completing his legal studies. O'Hagan, too, after the funeral had taken place and poetic tributes had been arranged,[53] turned his mind to legal studies. For him the shock of Davis's death was immense, perhaps even more than for Duffy. He was deeply devoted to Davis, and could not imagine life continuing as before without him. O'Hagan, who had been called to the Irish Bar in 1842, serving on the Munster circuit, now decided to pursue his earlier decision to study for the English Bar. O'Hagan informed the editor of *The Tablet*, Frederick Lucas, who lived in 25

---

51   LaRocca, op. cit., p. 33.
52   *Idem*, ref. to *Young Ireland*, pp. 750–53.
53   Among the tributes was a poem by O'Hagan's friend Denis MacCarthy. Also included were 'Sir Samuel Ferguson's splendid elegy and John Fisher Murray's stately verses' – editor, *Irish Monthly*, February 1903, p. 67.

Pembroke Square in London, of his plans. Their earlier acquaintance had grown into a friendship, as is evident from Lucas's undated reply:

> Your letter gave me a real pleasure, and your speaking
> of October as the month which is to bring you to Saxon
> land a pleasure still more real if possible. I anticipate
> your visit with more delight than I can easily express;
> and, so far as my occupations and very limited means
> permit, I hope you will allow me the honour – for it is
> an honour to serve those we love – to be of use to you
> in every way in my power.[54]

Student of Conveyancing

Having arranged for his books and papers to be looked after in preparation for a prolonged absence, O'Hagan set out for London in October 1845, a month after Davis's death.[55] Soon after his arrival he joined his friend John Pigot, who had preceded him to Lincoln's Inns, and there they both studied conveyancing under Peter Bellingar Brodie, perhaps the most eminent conveyancer of the age.[56]

Little is known of the two friends while they lived and studied in London. Many years later, in his *Conversations with Carlyle* (1892), Duffy recounted a seemingly insignificant incident involving O'Hagan, Pigot and himself in 1845. They were on a visit to the London home of Thomas Carlyle and his wife Jane, in order to defend the Irish and Irish nationalism against the attacks Carlyle had made in several of his works, including *Chartism*. During the visit, O'Hagan's nose began to bleed profusely, until the flow was eventually stemmed by using his pocket handkerchief. Nothing further is reported, but as a result of this visit and confrontation, Carlyle became a friend of Duffy and of others involved in *The Nation*.

Apart from Duffy's report of this event, which must have been an embarrassing memory for him, there is only one other reference to O'Hagan's time in London. It comes in the form of a remarkable

---

54 Lucas – O'Hagan, cit. M. Russell, 'Poets I have Known: John O'Hagan', in *Irish Monthly*, February 1903, pp. 64–5.
55 *Idem*, p. 67.
56 *Idem*. Peter Bellingar Brodie (1778–1854), in addition to being an outstanding conveyancer, also wrote on that and other related topics. (Conveyancing is concerned with the transfer of the legal title of property from one person to another.)

tribute written by Pigot, his friend and fellow student who knew him best during those years abroad.

Pigot's Memorandum

John Pigot was born on 28 February 1822, in Kilworth, near Fermoy, in County Cork. He was the eldest son of a barrister, David Richard Pigot, who would later become Chief Baron of the Exchequer. John, a gifted musician, met the future Young Irelanders through the Historical Society at Trinity College, where he counted O'Hagan, John Blake Dillon and Thomas Davis among his friends. As well as writing for *The Nation*, where he used the pseudonym 'Fermoy', he collected Irish airs with the encouragement of Davis, and indeed continued to add to his expansive collection even in London. He was a pall-bearer at Davis's funeral before going to England, where he arrived shortly before O'Hagan. When publishing the Memorandum in the *Irish Monthly* in February 1903, the editor, Matthew Russell, noted that it had 'never before been in print'.

'In October, 1845,' Pigot wrote, 'I returned to London. John O'Hagan also went there in the winter to study conveyancing in the same chambers where I was and which I did not leave till Christmas. He and I lodged together for six months – the only time during which I ever felt comfortable in any degree in London.' Pigot went on to express how his friendship with O'Hagan had made him a better person morally, intellectually and religiously (as already quoted in the Introduction to this book), before continuing in the same vein:

Many and many a time has he confirmed my wavering – shattered the creeping excuses and sophisms of my vanity and worldly pride – and taught me so sweetly the lessons of obedience to God and His Holy Church that, frequently when I left him to go up to bed, it was with tears in my eyes, and my first prayer on kneeling down was for grace to profit by his teaching and copy his example as nearly as I could. His fault may be over-scrupulousness at times – but that is unlikely to be ever my fault. I had been better and happier could I have taught myself John's quiet, earnest solemnity of contemplation, and busied myself more, as he does, with the great question of our salvation. But this can only come of God's grace, and John would tell it were wrong to despair of it.[57]

Tensions in Ireland

While O'Hagan and Pigot were settling in London, Gavan Duffy was endeavouring to strengthen *The Nation* after the loss of Davis. He engaged John Mitchel as manager and later as chief writer, enticed Thomas D'Arcy McGee,[58] a trained journalist, from London, and introduced Thomas Francis Meagher to the paper.[59] All of these formed the backbone of what Duffy termed the second Young Ireland party.[60] These developments led to what O'Hagan feared, however: that without Davis to hold them together, Young Ireland would lose its way and break with O'Connell.

The death of Duffy's young wife, Emily, took place shortly after that of Davis, and in the aftermath of these losses Duffy retired to lodgings in the Dublin hills to work on a book about the 1641 insurrection. In the meantime, he placed Mitchel in charge of *The Nation*. He was called back before long, however, to deal with labour problems about the printing of *The Nation* and to face unease about Mitchel's way of running the paper. In April 1846, O'Hagan wrote to Duffy expressing concern at the increasingly violent tone of *The Nation*, urging him to resume immediate control of the paper and to focus attention on the famine that was destroying the country.[61] Duffy seems to have been content with a mild response

---

57 *Irish Monthly,* February 1903, p. 65.
58 Thomas D'Arcy McGee (1825–1868) was an Irish nationalist and Canadian conservative. At the age of seventeen he went to the US, obtained work as a journalist, returned to Ireland in 1845, and worked for *The Nation* as lead writer. Involved in the 1848 rebellion, he escaped to America, and then moved to Canada in 1857, where he became active in politics, bringing about a confederation between those of Irish Catholic descent and those of British Protestant background. He served in government, and in 1867 was elected to the first Canadian parliament. He was assassinated in 1868 and given a state funeral. There are many memorials to his name in Ireland and Canada.
59 Thomas Francis Meagher (1823–1867), an Irish nationalist, was born in Waterford, took part in the rising of 1848, and was transported to Van Diemen's Land. He escaped to the US, studied law and joined the army at the start of the Civil War. He rose to the rank of brigadier general, having recruited and led the Irish Brigade. Later, he became governor of Montana. He drowned in the Missouri river in 1867.
60 Gavan Duffy, *Four Years of Irish History 1845–1849* (London: Cassell, 1883), pp. 6–14, cit. LaRocca, op. cit., pp. 36–7.
61 O'Hagan – Duffy, April 1846, Duffy Papers, cit. LaRocca, op. cit., p. 42.

to O'Hagan's advice. He reminded Mitchel that insurrections were not made to order in the back office of a newspaper, that the clergy were not in agreement with such views, and that military leaders with the required knowledge and skill were not available for such an enterprise.[62]

Despite Duffy's caution, Mitchel persisted with his aggressive writing,[63] with the result that the central committee of the Repeal Association banned *The Nation* from its reading rooms. O'Hagan, concerned by the militant tone of the publication, watched proceedings with a mixture of sadness and anger. Then, in the summer of 1846, O'Connell finally confronted Young Ireland. His demand that violence could never be used in the quest for Irish independence led to the secession of Young Irelanders at the meeting. Surprisingly, perhaps, O'Hagan supported his colleagues in their action. In the overheated political situation, loyalty to one's friends was expected, and their esteem was important to him.

O'Hagan does not seem to have been active in subsequent events, although he was present on 13 January 1847 at the formal establishment of the Irish Confederation by the seceders. This was a political organisation which, it was envisaged, would have a presence throughout the country by means of local clubs. It aimed at achieving a Home Rule government, assisting tenant farmers and the labouring classes by protecting their rights, diffusing knowledge about agriculture, and spreading an appreciation of Ireland's history among the people. The Confederates' policy was initially popular, but with the death of O'Connell in May 1847, a reaction set in against Young Ireland, and in the general election that summer, the Confederation fared badly.

Other Concerns

At this stage, O'Hagan's main focus was on his legal studies, although he typically found time for other interests too. Two of these in particular deserve attention here.

By the autumn of 1847, O'Hagan seems to have become weighed

---

62 Duffy – Mitchel, April 1846, Duffy Papers, cit. LaRocca, ibid.
63 In *The Nation*, May 1846, cit. LaRocca, ibid.

down by the gravity of the Famine and the country's many social problems. He joined with a group of barristers, churchmen, aristocrats and politicians in founding The Statistical and Social Inquiry Society of Ireland (SSISI).[64] At the time, societies using statistics as a mechanism to investigate social questions were very much in vogue in Britain, continental Europe and the US. In the Irish society, the earliest papers indicate an interest in analysing the causes of the Famine and making recommendations about transforming the Irish economy. In subsequent years, the society's agenda was extensive: changing the land law, reforming the Poor Law, proposing the more humane treatment of needy children, and promoting temperance. In its operation, the society maintained a relatively low profile. Insofar as it lobbied for changes in the law, it eschewed the organisation of mass protests or public meetings in favour of direct contacts with senior politicians and administrators, or by sending leaflets to Irish MPs.

It is an indication of the pragmatic nature of O'Hagan's nationalism that he worked closely with the other members of this society, the majority of whom were more in favour of British administration in Ireland than of Home Rule. What united them was their conviction that it was necessary to work with the Irish-based British administration, since many of the key decisions relating to Ireland rested with the politicians and senior officials in Dublin Castle. Indeed, many of the latter were members of the society, or were their close acquaintances. O'Hagan's situation was made easier by the constitution of the society, which precluded discussions of any topic that related to politics or religion.[65] He was to be president of the society in the final year of his life.

O'Hagan's close contact with people of different religious and political views did not deter him from speaking out strongly in support of another issue: the question of a Catholic university. He argued in favour of a university adapted to the requirements of the majority

---

64 The SSISI is still active, 175 years later.
65 Much of the information about the Statistical and Social Inquiry Society derives from an introduction to a book by M. E. Daly, *The Spirit of Earnest Inquiry: The Statistical and Social Inquiry Society of Ireland, 1847–1997* (Institute of Public Administration of Ireland, 1997).

population, taking issue with the suitability for Catholics of the only established university in Ireland at the time, Trinity College. While O'Hagan had made many friends in Trinity, as has been noted, and was a successful graduate of the university, he nevertheless argued strongly that it was an inappropriate environment for Catholics. His criticism appeared in the *Dublin Review*, in a review article on Denis Caulfield Heron's *Constitutional History of the University of Dublin* (1847). Nearly sixty years later the article was reissued by the Catholic Truth Society of Ireland as a pamphlet, under the title, *Trinity College – No Place for Catholics.*[66]

As Pigot's memorandum made clear, O'Hagan was an intellectually convinced and committed Catholic, not vehement in his views, but ready to defend or expound them as required. With radical friends he often argued against the complete separation of Church and state, maintaining that religion played an important role in the life of the national community and should be encouraged by the state. In the face of those who berated the Catholic Church for its 'intolerance', he argued that in the nineteenth century the Church was much more likely to be the victim than the perpetrator of persecution.[67] Putting his Christian faith into practice, O'Hagan worked for the poor during much of his life as a member of the St Vincent de Paul Society and in other charitable concerns as well. Already aware of the impending famine, as the letter to Duffy quoted above indicates, O'Hagan must have become aware of its true horrors during his time on the Munster circuit during 1847 ('Black' 47'), no doubt reinforcing his conviction about the futility of a revolution that would depend on the militant support of a starved and exhausted people.

A Failed Rebellion

Around this time, Duffy and Mitchel had a parting of the ways. Mitchel withdrew from *The Nation*, explaining later that he had come to see 'as absolutely necessary a more vigorous policy against

---

66 Cit. in 'Judge O'Hagan. 'Some Notes on his Life and Letters', in *Irish Monthly,* August 1912, p. 406.
67 Sinéad Sturgeon and James Quinn, 'O'Hagan, John', in *Dictionary of Irish Biography*, op. cit.

the English government than that which William Smith O'Brien,[68] Charles Gavan Duffy and other Young Ireland leaders were willing to pursue'.[69] On 12 February 1848, he published the first issue of his own newspaper, *The United Irishman*. In its editorial he announced to the Lord Lieutenant of Ireland, Lord Clarendon, that the purpose of the journal was 'to sweep this island clean of the English name and nation'.[70] He also supported the proposals enunciated by James Fintan Lalor[71] in favour of a revolution that would have the land as its rallying cry, believing that the people would rally if land rather than Repeal was the issue. Mitchel appeared to trust that there would be a spontaneous rebellion once the flag was raised, but seemed to have no clear idea how the leaders would be recruited or how sufficient arms would be acquired.

Like O'Hagan, Duffy considered these plans to be unrealistic. Nevertheless, when a revolution took place in France in February 1848, leading to the abdication of King Louis-Philippe, Duffy trumpeted in *The Nation*, 'We must unite, we must act … If needs be we must die rather than let this providential hour pass over us as unliberated.'[72] On 22 April, the British government passed the Treason Felony Act, 1848, and Mitchel was arrested and sentenced to be transported to Van Diemen's Land for fourteen years. In July, Duffy was arrested and the production machinery of *The Nation* was seized, but he escaped conviction. Later that month, on 29 July, William Smith O'Brien, Thomas Francis Meagher and about a hundred Confeder-

---

68 William Smith O'Brien (1803–1864) was an Irish nationalist, descended from the eleventh-century Irish High King, Brian Boru. He was elected to parliament and became a leader in the Young Ireland movement. Arrested for sedition for his part in the 1848 rising, he was sentenced to Van Diemen's Land. Released in 1854 on condition that he would not return to Ireland, he spent two years in Brussels until he received a full pardon in 1856. He returned to Ireland but took no further part in politics.

69 Cit. in 'John Mitchel', *Wikipedia*.

70 *Idem.*

71 James Fintan Lalor (1807–1849) was an Irish social revolutionary and political essayist in *The Nation* and *Irish Felon* newspapers. He was in prison during the rising of 1848, but was involved in another failed attempt at revolution in Tipperary and Waterford in 1849. His rhetoric in the *Irish Felon* on 1 July 1848 stirred generations of nationalists: 'We hold the present government and all existing rights of property on our soil to be mere usurpation and tyranny … and our purpose is to abolish them entirely, or lose our lives in the attempt … We owe no obedience to laws enacted by another nation without our consent, nor respect the assumed rights of property which are starving and exterminating our people.'

72 Cit. LaRocca, op. cit., p. 68.

ates took part in a rebellion, unsuccessfully engaging some forty policemen near Ballingarry, County Tipperary. O'Brien and Meagher were arrested and sentenced to be hanged, drawn and quartered. The sentence was subsequently commuted to penal exile for life.

O'Hagan, who was probably busy completing his legal studies in London, was not involved in these developments. It is likely that he was back in Dublin in 1846 to join Duffy in celebrating his second marriage, to Susan Hughes, a highly cultured woman who had studied music under Franz Liszt and Frédéric Chopin, and who was also his first cousin.[73] It is also likely that O'Hagan visited Duffy in Newgate Prison in July 1848. What is certain is that he was back in Ireland by November 1848, when he acted with Sir Samuel Ferguson[74] in the successful legal defence of Young Irelander Richard D'Alton Williams.[75] Together with Sir Colman O'Loghlen,[76] O'Hagan assisted Isaac Butt[77] in defending Duffy during his prolonged trial. This trial occasioned much public interest. Despite a strong government case and a packed jury, agreement on a verdict could not be reached and, following a retrial in April 1849, a non-guilty verdict was handed down with a vote for Duffy's acquittal.[78]

73 Cit. LaRocca, op. cit., p.82.
74 Samuel Ferguson (1810–1886) was born in Belfast, but spent most of his life in Dublin. He became celebrated as poet, antiquarian, barrister and public servant. His collected poems, *Lays of the Western Gael*, was published in 1865, and was followed by an honorary doctorate from Trinity College, Dublin University. He wrote in both Irish and English. He retired from the bar in 1867 and was appointed First Deputy Keeper of the Public Records Office of Ireland. He was knighted in 1878. His major work, published after his death, was *Ogham Inscriptions in Ireland*.
75 Richard D'Alton Williams (1827–1862) was an Irish nationalist and poet. He commenced his medical studies in Trinity College Dublin in 1843, and was instrumental in founding the Society of St Vincent de Paul in Ireland. Having joined Young Ireland and the Confederates, he was arrested in 1848 and charged with treason, but he was successfully defended by Sir Samuel Ferguson and John O'Hagan. He qualified in medicine in Edinburgh in 1849 and later emigrated to the US.
76 Sir Colman O'Loghlen (1819–1877) was an Irish baronet, lawyer and politician. Born in County Clare, he was elected to the House of Commons for Clare 1863–77. He held the office of Judge Advocate General, a political office. On his death his title passed to his brother Bryan, premier of Victoria, Australia.
77 Isaac Butt (1813–1879) was an Irish lawyer and politician. Professor of Political Economy in Dublin University (Trinity College), 1836–41, he was called to the Irish Bar in 1838. A member of parliament from 1852, he made Irish Home Rule a political slogan and was president of the Home Rule Confederation of Great Britain, 1873–77, until superseded by the young Parnell.
78 Duffy, *Four Years of Irish History*, op. cit., pp. 743–45, 755, cit. LaRocca, op. cit.,pp. 92–94.

Changing Friendships

In subsequent years, Duffy was actively committed to constitutional reform. In August 1850, he was involved in the foundation of the Irish Tenant League which encompassed both Catholics and Protestants working together in defence of tenant rights. In the general election of 1852, Duffy was elected for New Ross and, together with almost fifty Irish liberal MPs committed to the principle of independent opposition, took his seat in Westminster.

Divisions soon arose, however, and Duffy, now in poor health and quite dispirited, resigned from the Tenant League in 1854, and sold his interest in *The Nation* to A. M. Sullivan and Michael Clery.[79] With the help of a friend, he cleared the debts incurred by his public life,[80] and in October 1855 sailed for Australia with his wife and three of his children.[81] For O'Hagan, who had kept in touch with Duffy and his family over the years, their departure for distant shores left a gap in his life.

From the friends of his student days, there remained the socially active John Pigot and Denis Florence MacCarthy. Pigot, it appears, was no longer as close to O'Hagan in the 1850s as in former years. A handsome, gregarious young man, he did much to win support for Young Ireland in Dublin's fashionable circles. In politics, he had become increasingly critical of O'Connell, and resigned from the Repeal Association in September 1845. Following his return from England in 1847, his views became quite militant. He insisted that there could be no compromise between the Repeal Association and the Confederation (the Young Irelanders who had broken from the Repeal Association), and he acted as military correspondent of *The Nation*, where he published articles on guerrilla warfare. He was out of the country at the time of the 1848 rising, either for reasons of

---

79 A. M. Sullivan (1829–1884) was born in Bantry, County Cork. An Irish nationalist and artist, he was assistant editor of *The Nation* in 1850, becoming editor and co-proprietor with Michael Clery. With his brother, T. D. Sullivan, he made the paper a potent factor in the nationalist cause, 1861–64. Called to the Irish Bar in 1876, he was made QC in 1881, and elected MP for Louth from 1874 to 1880. As a member of Dublin Corporation he acquired the site for the Grattan monument in College Green, Dublin. He was author of two books: *New Ireland* (1877) and *The Story of Ireland* (1883). Michael Clery was a Dublin businessman in 1855, and became sole proprietor of *The Nation* in 1858.

80 Duffy, *My Life in Two Hemispheres*, p. 123, cit. LaRocca, op. cit., p. 130.

81 Ibid.

health or at the behest of his father. Back in Ireland later that year, he was part of William Smith O'Brien's defence team during the state trials that continued into 1849. At that time, he would undoubtedly have met up again with the 'quiet contemplative' O'Hagan, who was defending Duffy.

In the 1850s and into the 1860s, Pigot led a busy and varied public life. He was elected to the Royal Irish Academy in 1851 and was active in the Society for the Preservation and Publication of the Melodies of Ireland. He served as treasurer of the Celtic Society, was a member of the Irish Archaeological Society, a co-founder of the Royal Hibernian Society, and belonged to a committee that aimed at the publication of an Irish language dictionary. In 1853 he wrote a memorandum proposing the establishment of the National Art Gallery of Ireland and was a founding member of that institution in 1864. He was also active in establishing the Irish Academy of Music (later the Royal Irish Academy of Music). It is not clear how much he and O'Hagan kept in touch during these years, but it can legitimately be presumed that O'Hagan followed Pigot's career with interest, supported his activities in so far as he could, and rejoiced at his many initiatives and successes.

Of all his old friends during those years, O'Hagan was closest to MacCarthy. In the 1850s and into the early 1860s, he frequently discussed with him his prevailing interest in poetry and literature, and he was a familiar visitor to MacCarthy's house on Killiney Hill in County Dublin. MacCarthy continued to write and publish poetry and works of translation right up to the end of his life in 1882. He became the first Professor of English in the Catholic University of Ireland under John Henry Newman in the 1850s.

CHAPTER 7

Career Success and Inner Search

A Modest Lifestyle

During the 1850s, O'Hagan gave increasing attention to his legal work, but he managed to pursue his other interests as well, particularly when he was on the Munster circuit. Many years later, Matthew Russell recorded that 'when he [O'Hagan] wrote to congratulate Mr Justice James Murphy on his elevation to the bench, the judge in his reply recalled their first circuits together, and how they had striven to raise the tone of conversation at the dinners by promoting an interest in Shakespeare and other intellectual topics'.[82]

From the 1850s, O'Hagan concentrated mostly on equity law. As time passed and his reputation spread, he was involved in cases attracting higher fees, but his preference was for a quiet, modest lifestyle. An instance of his preference for a life away from the limelight was illustrated in September 1850, when he contributed to the *Dublin Review* an unsigned essay of considerable weight on the writings of Thomas Carlyle. Many years later, James Anthony Froude,[83] in his *Thomas Carlyle: a History of His Life in London* (vol. ii, p. 65), recalled Carlyle's own reaction to this article: 'A review in the *Dublin Review* he found "excellently serious" and conjectured that it came from some Anglican convert or pervert. It was written I believe by Dr Ward.'[84] It was written, in fact, by the twenty-eight-year-old John

---

82 Editor, *Irish Monthly*, August 1912, 'Judge O'Hagan, Some Notes on his Life and Letters', p. 427.

83 J. A. Froude (1818–1894) was a historian, novelist and biographer. A fiercely polemical writer, his controversial works include *Thomas Carlyle: A History of His Life in London, 1834–1881* (1882) and his celebrated *History of England from the Fall of Wolsey to the Defeat of the Spanish Armada* (1862). Cf. *Irish Monthly*, August 1912, loc. cit., p. 427.

84 Dr William George Ward (1812–1882) was an Anglican scholar, belonged to the Tractarian group in Oxford, and became a Roman Catholic 1845. A trenchant writer with strong views, he was Professor of Philosophy at St Edmund's College, Ware. A regular contributor to *The Dublin Review*, he was its editor from 1863–78. A strong defender of traditional Catholic teaching and an opponent of liberal Catholicism, he vigorously supported the promulgation of the dogma of papal infallibility in 1870.

O'Hagan. Although he was only five years a barrister at the time, his work clearly impressed Carlyle and, it would appear, even Froude himself.

In the early 1850s, O'Hagan found time to stay in touch with his friends and follow their careers. His close friendship with MacCarthy has already been mentioned, and he kept up contact with Duffy too. O'Hagan must have rejoiced at the news of John Mitchel's escape from Van Diemen's Land on 19 July 1853. In January 1850, O'Hagan welcomed the decision of his good friend, Frederick Lucas, to move the publication of *The Tablet* to Dublin. A few years later, however, on 22 October 1855, he received what was perhaps the saddest news of the decade for him: the death of Lucas at the age of forty-three.

It was perhaps the loss of two such close friends in the one month – Duffy to exile and Lucas to death – that prompted O'Hagan shortly afterwards to take stock of his life and spend eight days apart in a silent retreat.

Time of Retreat

O'Hagan's retreat was based on the Spiritual Exercises of St Ignatius Loyola, founder of the Jesuits. Ignatius explains in his introductory notes that, just as physical exercises are used to improve the body, so spiritual exercises are designed to strengthen the inner life of the retreatant, who is encouraged to approach them 'with an open and generous heart' in order to find out God's plan for him/her. Originally intended to take place over thirty days or so, the Spiritual Exercises were frequently adapted to a shorter period of time, typically eight days, for those unable to devote a whole month to them. They are particularly helpful for someone endeavouring to make a life decision, but it is not clear if this was what prompted O'Hagan to embark on these eight days of prayer and silence.

The Exercises follow a clear if flexible pattern. They commence with an introductory reflection on the purpose of life and its implications for the individual. The main body of the Exercises is then divided into four adaptable periods of time known as 'weeks'. The first 'week' is spent reviewing the obstacles that stand in the way of the retreatant following God's plan. In O'Hagan's summary in his retreat notes, he recorded how he examined his life by dividing it into four periods: '1. From 8 years to 15; 2. from 15–23; 3. from 23 to the year 1850; 4. from 1850 to the present time'.

The retreat programme then goes on to consider how God chooses to send his Son, Jesus Christ, into the world, to live as a human among humans and to lead them to God. The rest of the retreat then involves the retreatant spending time on the Gospel accounts of the life of Christ, from his infancy through to his death and resurrection, using the imagination to enter into the experience of these events. Everything is aimed at helping the retreatant to get to know Christ more personally, to awaken a response of love, and to evoke a desire to follow more closely in his footsteps. The retreat concludes on a note of gratitude, confident in Jesus' promise to be with his followers until the end of time.

It is significant that, judging from his notes, one meditation that stood out for O'Hagan was that on the hidden life of Christ. O'Hagan pondered how Jesus spent the greater part of his life as a carpenter, with his mother as an ordinary housewife, and Joseph as his teacher in his own trade and in the Jewish law. That this hidden life was perfectly acceptable to God clearly resonated with something deep in O'Hagan.

From the sixteenth century to the present time, men and women of all classes have beneffited spiritually and morally from the Spiritual Exercises, sometimes to a remarkable degree. In many instances they have experienced notable, even dramatic, changes in their lives. The benefits of the retreat to John O'Hagan were known to himself alone, but those days of peace, prayer and reflection surely helped him to cope with the loss of his close friends and to face the future with renewed confidence. In fact, some notable changes did appear around this time, from the end of the 1850s. While O'Hagan remained nationalist in his sympathies, he quietly put behind him his links with the political aspects of Young Ireland; he began to consider the prospect of marriage; and he started to devote himself more and more to his four main interests (not necessarily in order): poetry, religion, education and law.

Part 2 (1856–90)
Educator, High Court Judge, Poet

Chapter 8

Gifted Speaker and University Professor

Honouring Thomas Moore

O'Hagan's quiet life was interrupted in October 1857, when he was invited to be one of the speakers at the unveiling of a statue to honour the Irish poet, Thomas Moore.[85] Moore's work was popular in Ireland, while it was known and celebrated abroad as well. The unveiling of his statue at the junction of College Street and Westmoreland Street was a major cause for celebration.

On 17 October, Sydney Inwood Jones, who was present at the inauguration, wrote to her aunt, the popular author, Lady Morgan,[86] describing the occasion and remarking on the speeches in particular.

Including ladies and gentlemen, she estimated that there were about 6,000 people present, a better-behaved 'mob' than would be found in England. The speakers addressed the crowd from a little circle, at the centre of which was Lord Carlyle. Inwood Jones described the speeches vividly:

Lord Charlemont spoke with feeling and good taste;
Lord Carlisle's (sic) speech was all poetry and pathos, and was charmingly delivered ... but the speaker of the day, out

85   Thomas Moore (1779–1852) was an Irish poet, lyricist, satirist and political propagandist. A graduate of Trinity College (Dublin University), he studied law in London, and was a close friend of Lord Byron and Shelley. His poem 'Lalla Rookh' (1817) earned him the highest price ever paid by an English publisher (£3,000) and was the most translated poem of its time. His major poetic work was *Irish Melodies (1807–34)*, a group of 130 poems to be sung to Irish tunes as arranged by Sir John Stevenson. These were frequently performed for the London aristocracy and aroused sympathy and support for the Irish nationalists, who looked to Moore as a hero. A lifelong supporter of the Catholic cause, he courageously wrote a biography of Lord Edward FitzGerald (1831), a leader of the 1798 rebellion.

86   Sydney Inwood Jones – Lady Morgan, 17 October 1857, in *Lady Morgan's Memoirs: Autobiography, Diaries and Correspondence* (revised, 2 vols., London, 1863). Sydney Morgan (née Owenson) was born in Dublin about the year 1780, and became a popular novelist and a supporter of Catholic Emancipation. In 1812 she married Sir Thomas Charles Morgan MD, who died in 1843. She received a civil list pension in recognition of her services to literature. She died in London in 1859.

and out for eloquence and extraordinary oratorical powers (such as I never heard, and could only imagine Grattan's or Curran's to have been) was Mr O'Hagan's! It was perfectly astounding. Now I understand what is called Irish eloquence. The immense flow of words of the best language, gave one the idea that his imagination was overflowing. It was extraordinary.[87]

This testimony to O'Hagan's eloquence might lead us to consider the identity of one of the characters in the 'Aeolus' episode of James Joyce's *Ulysses*: 'Where have you a man now at the bar like those fellows, like Whiteside, like Isaac Butt, like silver-tongued O'Hagan?' It seems possible that it was John O'Hagan whom Joyce had in mind, rather than his contemporary, Thomas O'Hagan, who served as Lord Chancellor for Ireland on two occasions.

Mention of Joyce evokes the name of John Henry Newman, whom Joyce admired, and who was the first rector of the Catholic University in Dublin. Newman became an important figure for O'Hagan, finding in him a friend to be revered.

The Catholic University

The Queen's Colleges, as noted earlier, divided opinion in Ireland, being supported in principle by the Young Irelanders but denounced as 'Godless colleges' by O'Connell and his followers. They finally opened their doors to students in Belfast, Cork and Galway at the end of October 1849, but the following year, at the national synod in Thurles (22 August–10 September) the bishops decreed that the Queen's Colleges were to be avoided by faithful Catholics 'because of grave and intrinsic dangers'.[88] Under the leadership of Archbishop Paul Cullen, and with the approval of Pope Pius IX, the bishops embarked on a plan to provide a university for the Catholic population. To give standing to the new institution, they invited the celebrated Oxford churchman and convert to Catholicism, John Henry Newman, to act as rector of the new university.

---

87 *Italics* as in text.
88 T. W. Moody, F. X. Martin, F. J. Byrne, *A New History of Ireland,* vol. viii (Oxford: Oxford University Press, 2011), p. 328.

Newman envisaged the university becoming an academic centre for Catholics across the English-speaking world, and this vision aroused the interest of a section of the educated middle class, including former Young Irelanders O'Hagan, Pigot and MacCarthy. It is likely that O'Hagan attended at least some of Newman's lectures, entitled 'Discourses on the Scope and Nature of University Education', which were delivered at the Rotunda in Dublin in 1852. These lectures, revised and extended, would later be published and widely read as *The Idea of a University*. The Catholic University, with Newman as rector, opened on 3 November 1854.

That year, and into the next, the university was in 'a provisional state' as Newman sought to finalise arrangements and appoint teaching staff. The first recorded meeting between Newman and O'Hagan took place on 27 April 1854, when Newman noted in an attachment to a letter: 'Dined at Kingstown with Mr J. B. O'Ferral meeting J. O'Hagan and H. W. [Wilberforce]'.[89] Newman, it appears, was seeking possible lecturers for the university and had been given O'Hagan's name. Shortly afterwards, in his 'University Journal' for 18 May 1854, Newman noted that 'Mr O'Hagan has today accepted the professorship of Political Economy (I offered him the choice of that and Philosophical Law)'.[90] Subsequently, O'Hagan made his position clear regarding his acceptance: 'I cannot promise to begin at once, but you may set me down on the understanding I have a year for preparation.'[91]

It is clear that, by July 1854, O'Hagan had become someone to consult. On 19 July, Newman instructed Robert Ormsby, Professor of Classical Literature, whom he knew from their Oxford connections, to 'learn from John O'Hagan something of the turn of mind of Mr MacCarthy ... If he were a person to take up the cause of literature generally, I should like to make good use of him, if he would be

89 Charles Stephen Dessain, *The Letters and Diaries of John Henry Newman, January 1854 – September 1855*, vol xvi, p. 117n. Many of Newman's letters cited in the text are from this great work of Dessain: vols. i-vi (Oxford, 1978–84), vols xi-xxii (London, 1961–72) and vols xxii-xxxi (Oxford, 1973–77)]. Henry Wilberforce (1807–1873)) was a former Oxford student and a close friend of Newman. Formerly a Church of England clergyman and Tractarian, he became a Roman Catholic in 1850.
90 *Idem*, p. 135, n. 2.
91 Mentioned in Newman – Aubrey de Vere, 21 August 1854, *idem*, pp. 232–3. Aubrey de Vere was a noted poet, who lived at the family demesne in County Limerick.

used.'[92] Ormsby subsequently reported that MacCarthy was 'mainly a literary man,' but he had 'a remarkably painstaking and industrious mind, and ... a good deal of real genius'.[93] Denis MacCarthy was subsequently appointed lecturer in poetry at the university.

On 23 August, writing from Birmingham to the secretary of the university, Thomas Scratton, Newman requested him to seek 'some good information' about 'Mr Butler, the mathematician', and then asked, 'Does John O'Hagan know him? Who can definitely speak of him?'[94] Scratton obtained positive reports from Butler's former tutor at Trinity College, Dublin, and Butler was duly named Professor of Mathematics.[95]

Tensions with the Archbishop

At this time, the Oratory in Birmingham, which Newman had founded, was struggling for its survival, making it necessary for him to commute frequently between Dublin and Birmingham. His many absences caused unease among the bishops, especially Archbishop Cullen, who was the main link between the episcopacy and the Rector of the University. Cullen also sought at times to influence Newman in his choice of faculty members, leading to further tension between the two. Newman, looking for greater independence in his administration of the university, told Cullen on 1 October 1854 that 'the bishops must put confidence in me ... I must have my arms free'.[96]

In January 1855, Cullen's personal and political views clearly influenced the following recommendation he made to Newman: 'I trust you will make every exertion to keep the university free from Young Irelandism, of which the spirit is so evident in *The Nation*.'[97] In response, Newman replied carefully but firmly:

> I trust most earnestly that politics will not come into the University. If they do, it will be utterly against my wish. There are persons such as Mr John O'Hagan who (I have

92 Newman – Ormsby, 19 July 1854, op. cit., p. 199. Italics in text.
93 Ormsby report, op. cit., p. 199, fn. 3
94 Newman – Scratton, 23 August 1854, op. cit., p. 232.
95 Op. cit. p. 232, fn. 1.
96 Newman – Cullen, 1 October 1854, op. cit., pp. 263–4.
97 Cullen – Newman, 12 January 1855, op. cit.. p. 359, n.2.

been told) once were called Young Irelanders – all I know is, that they are admirable persons now, and, I am sure, would show nothing of the spirit of which your Grace complains so justly. I may meet with others as far from any political spirit now, who once had the name – and if so, should they be eligible men, I do not see the harm of employing them – but I feel deeply that we shall be ruined, if we let politics in.[98]

Concerned about his relationship with Cullen, Newman wrote to a trusted friend, Bishop David Moriarty of Kerry, on 29 April 1855, asking his opinion of John Pigot. Newman explained that Pigot had promised him 'to entertain the prospect of lecturing on Real Property', but he was aware that his political views might not concur with Cullen's. Moriarty answered in no uncertain manner:

I do not at all share in Dr Cullen's distrust of those he calls Young Irelanders ... but whatever estimate is to be made of them Pigot cannot be ranked among those Dr Cullen would distrust. He is a truly estimable young man, working quietly at his profession – In obedience to his father he withdrew from his political party in '47, and never that I remember took part in politics since.[99]

By 3 October 1854, Newman was able to present to the bishops his list of interim appointments for the School of Arts, which included O'Hagan in Political Economy. Writing to Scratton on 28 May 1855, Newman mentioned O'Hagan and two others as due to give inaugural lectures 'for the first three weeks of June'; then, almost a month later, on 26 June, he directed that 'De Vere, Pollen, O'Hagan ought (I suppose) to have £5 a piece for their Inaugural Lectures.'[100]

Cullen's predecessor as Archbishop of Dublin, Daniel Murray,[101] had rightly anticipated the problem of funding the university. Limited finances and how to manage them effectively proved to be a major issue from the start. In addition, the absence of state recognition of its degrees inevitably had an adverse impact on student numbers and

98 Newman – Cullen, 24 January 1855, op. cit., pp. 358–9.
99 Moriarty – Newman, *idem*, p. 456, fn. 3.
100 Newman – Scratton, 28 May 1855, op. cit., p. 475, n. 1; and Newman – Scratton, 26 June 1855, op. cit., p. 494.
101 See T. J. Morrissey, *The Life and Times of Daniel Murray, Archbishop of Dublin 1823–1852* (Dublin: Messenger Publications, 2018), pp. 258f.

income, making the future of the university ever more precarious. Newman was concerned about the financial situation and the effect it was having on staff remuneration. On 17 November 1856, in a letter to Dr Laurence Forde, Professor of Canon Law, he acknowledged that he could not name a salary to him.[102] He added that 'Mr O'Hagan, Mr Pollen, and others have been paid just for the few lectures they have delivered.'[103]

In view of the difficulties he was experiencing in dealing with the hierarchy on money matters, Newman made several attempts to establish a lay finance committee for the university. On 20 June 1856, in a letter to Cullen, he outlined the structure of such a committee, revealing in the process his esteem for O'Hagan. The committee, Newman suggested, should have three members: one member from the university, and two external to it, adding that 'for the university member I propose Professor Butler or John O'Hagan'. For the other two positions he offered a list of seven names.[104] Once more, his efforts were thwarted. In fairness to Cullen and the bishops, it should be noted that their funds came from various sources, were meant to support many different causes, and were subject in many cases to Roman inspection. In addition, the reigning pope at that time, Pius IX, was particularly wary of lay activity, having himself been driven from Rome by a violent lay democracy. In the circumstances, the handing over of the finances of a Catholic university to a lay committee, however reliable, was unthinkable.

Meanwhile, Newman's preoccupation with the Oratory in Birmingham appeared to Cullen and some other prelates to be taking precedence over his obligations in Dublin. He was a frequent traveller between Birmingham and Dublin, and at times conducted the business of the university by letter. Indeed, the internal business of the Birmingham Oratory prompted him to visit some Oratory foundations in Sardinia, Lombardy and Tuscany, leading to his absence from the Catholic University from 12 December 1855 until the beginning of February 1856.[105]

102 It was Cullen, in fact, who refused to name a salary. Cf. Newman – Forde, 22 January 1857.
103 Newman – Forde, 17 November 1856, op. cit., vol. xvii, p. 451.
104 Newman – Cullen, 20 June 1856, op. cit., vol. xvii, p. 286 and n.1.
105 Ibid., p. 96.

Thoughts of Resignation

By October 1856, Newman was talking of resigning from the university 'at the end of the ensuing year'.[106] His intention became known to the academic staff, and, on 9 October 1856, O'Hagan wrote a letter to Newman on their behalf. This letter so moved Newman that he copied out the following extract for himself:

> All that you mention is hard and trying in the last degree.
> I fear your association in connection with Ireland will
> dwell very unpleasant in your memory, as of a country
> that never understood or appreciated you. Well – so far
> as regards the Irish professors in the university (I speak
> of those whom I know, the laymen) it is quite the
> opposite. We have always felt, that you only wanted
> power and freedom of action to make the institution
> march. It is painful not to be able to do anything beyond
> expressing sincere sympathy.[107]

From Birmingham, Newman replied with some affection:

> Thank you for your most kind letter. On the contrary, I have
> experienced nothing but kindness and attention, of which I
> am quite unworthy, from every class of persons in Ireland,
> whom I have come near. I make no exception, except Dr Cullen and Dr MacHale. To all other bishops I feel exceedingly
> grateful. If I don't use the word 'grateful' about the professors,
> it is because I should use much warmer and more intimate
> terms in speaking of them. I submit it as a mortification, intended to wean me from the world, that I am bound by duty
> here, and by my years, to separate myself from persons I love
> so much and from a work towhich all my human feelings so
> much incline me.[108]

Subsequently, at a celebration in honour of St Laurence O'Toole, Patron of the Dublin Archdiocese, O'Hagan joined with the Archbishop and with Dr Andrew Ellis[109] in speeches in honour of the

106 Newman – John Wallis, from Birmingham, 21 October 1856, op. cit., p. 414.
107 O'Hagan – Newman, 9 October 1856, *idem*, p. 415.
108 Newman – O'Hagan, 11 October 1856, *idem*, p. 483.

109 Dr Andrew Ellis was Professor in the Theory and Practice of Surgery in the Faculty of Medicine.

university. O'Hagan's speech was marked by the warmth with which he spoke of Newman, and he concluded by stating his belief that for centuries to come Newman, although an Englishman, would be spoken of with affection and pride as one of the greatest and most enduring benefactors of Ireland.[110]

On 2 December, Newman commented to Dr Dunne, who had informed him of O'Hagan's speech, 'He did me far too much honour and I put what he said to his extreme warmth of heart. Yet it is very pleasant indeed to know that he said it, while I know I don't deserve it – and I have no difficulty in confessing that Englishmen have deep reasons for shame when they think how they have treated Ireland.'[111]

In 1858, Newman was still rector of the university, although he was operating almost entirely from Birmingham. On 20 April of that year, in a letter to William Kirby Sullivan[112] about articles for the university's publication, *The Atlantis*, he rejoiced 'to hear of Mr O'Hagan's paper' on Joan of Arc.[113] A month later, on 30 May, writing again to Sullivan, he commented, 'Mr O'Hagan's article has come to me this morning. I like the look of it very much, and I am glad you are putting it first.'[114] Newman also knew that O'Hagan was busy with his university schedule: 'John O'Hagan has read, I suppose, 6 lectures. He has taken great pains with them, and he has had nothing for his professorship. I think he ought to have £7 a lecture, which will be 40 guineas.'[115]

O'Hagan was prepared to take on extra work too at Newman's behest. On 14 July, the latter wrote from Birmingham apologising for the delay in thanking O'Hagan 'for agreeing to add the professorship of Juris Prudence' to his 'present professorship'. He added, 'Will you tell me if it will be what you expect and are satisfied with, if I consid-

110 Dunne – Newman, 1 December 1856, op. cit., vol. xvii, p. 470, n.3.
111 Newman – Dunne, 2 December 1856, op. cit., p. 470.
112 William Kirby Sullivan (1822–1890) was a renowned chemist and an enthusiastic promoter of Irish industry. As Professor of Medical Chemistry in the Catholic University he edited *The Atlantis*, a science publication with a literary section.
113 Newman – W. K. Sullivan, 20 April 1858, op. cit., vol. xviii (April 1857–December 1858), p. 323, and n. 4.
114 Newman – Sullivan, 30 May 1858, vol. xviii, p. 360. The article was placed first in the July issue of *The Atlantis*. O'Hagan's interest in the subject may be related to his intense interest in medieval history, as evidenced by his later translation of *La Chanson de Roland*. The career of Joan of Arc remained an interest of O'Hagan's, leading to a book that his wife would publish posthumously in 1893.
115 Newman – Scratton, 28 June 1858, op. cit., p. 395.

er your regular salary of £200 to begin with the opening of next term i.e. the first payment is due on December 21.'[116]

O'Hagan's role as Professor of Jurisprudence was soon in question, however. On 28 September, Newman informed him, 'I have just received a letter from the Archbishop of Dublin. I am deeply anxious lest it should throw serious difficulties in the way of my fulfilling my engagement with you as to your professorship. It takes me quite by surprise. It is the first hint he has thrown out since I was Rector of the necessity of reducing the expenditure.'[117]

Newman was facing something of a conundrum, as he outlined in a postscript to a letter to Robert Ormsby: 'The Archbishops have told me I must reside a considerable time in Dublin. I feel a Rector ought to do so. I can't. Resignation then is all that remains.' In a further postscript he wrote, 'I have, since I wrote this, written to John O'Hagan, and told him what I have told you.'[118]

Resignation and Final Departure

On 12 November 1858, Newman wrote once again to Ormsby enclosing a copy of his resignation for the attention of the professors. 'It is right,' he wrote, 'that they should know my precise grounds for the act, and not be at the mercy of rumours and reports.' His resignation was 'a final act', he explained, for the majority of the archbishops were not disposed 'to grant what, even were I at liberty to make terms, which I am not, I certainly should require, for the good of the University'.[119]

The final recorded letter of Newman to John O'Hagan about the university was written two days later, mostly about business matters. O'Hagan's reply on 18 November is not extant, but Newman was so taken by it that he copied out the following part of it:[120] 'There is no use in saying anything, I suppose, on the subject of your resignation. Everything (as you once wrote to me) has no doubt its reason, but I cannot help deploring your loss, as a calamity to the coming gener-

---

116 Newman – O'Hagan, 14 July 1858, *idem*, p. 410. The £200 was made up of £100 for his present professorship, and £100 for the new professorship.
117 Newman – O'Hagan, 28 September 1858, *idem*, p. 468.
118 Newman – Ormsby, early October 1858, *idem*, p. 480, and the two postscripts.
119 Newman – Ormsby, 12 November 1858, op. cit., p. 512.
120 Newman – O'Hagan, 14 November 1858, op. cit., pp. 512–13.

ation of Irishmen.'[121]

This may have been the last of their correspondence about the university, but it was not the end of their friendship. After Newman finally settled in Birmingham, O'Hagan paid frequent visits to the Oratory,[122] and the two men exchanged further letters. Indeed, among the letters O'Hagan preserved were many from Newman that were remarkable for their affectionate tone, as in the following, sent from the Oratory on 3 March 1874:

> I have been exceedingly gratified, or rather have been much surprised and deeply touched by your letter, which has just come. I know I do not deserve it at all – but still I accept it with all my heart as if I were worthy of it, and do not mean to part with it. I know you will be led by what you say to remember me sometimes in your prayers, the benefit of which, as of those of all friends, I need so much now that I am so old. And I can say on my part that your name has all along been on my list of Irish friends, who were so kind and indulgent to me when I was with them, and claim my remembrance.[123]

This 'so old' man would live, in fact, for another fifteen years, into his ninetieth year. He died on 11 August 1890, just three months before O'Hagan's own death at the age of sixty-eight. O'Hagan, it would seem, looked up to Newman as someone to be admired and emulated for his gracious, assured manner, his store of learning, his deep spirituality, and his courtesy and respect for those who crossed his path.

121 O'Hagan – Newman, 18 November 1858. We learn of this from a comment attached to Newman's letter to O'Hagan of 14 November 1858, p. 513, and fn. 1.
122 Note in op. cit. under O'Hagan in 'Index of Persons and Places', p. 621.
123 Cit. M. Russell among some 'unpublished letters' in his 'Poets I have Known, No. 2. John O'Hagan', in *Irish Monthly*, February 1903, p. 78.

CHAPTER 9

Public Honours and Private Life

New Undertakings

A friend of O'Hagan's, Thomas MacNevin, used to say of him that, by moving in a new direction, he was constantly causing you to revise your judgement of him.[124] This might well be said of O'Hagan's whole life and career in the 1860s.

While attending to his expanding legal practice and continuing to lecture at the Catholic University, O'Hagan was busy with other projects as well. In 1860, he contributed an article to *The Atlantis* entitled, 'Views Preliminary to the Study of Political Economy'. The following year, he published a legal book, outside his specialisation in equity law, entitled *Punishment and Reform*. In that same year he was honoured to be offered the position of Commissioner for the Board of National Education, which he accepted. That he was offered this position implies that Cullen approved his appointment and had laid aside any suspicion he had of O'Hagan arising from his past as a Young Irelander.

In 1864, O'Hagan was again honoured by being appointed Chairman of the Court of Quarter Sessions for County Westmeath, a position he held until 1870. This title carried with it judicial status and responsibility without any formal appointment as judge. In that same year he became involved in the Afternoon Lectures on Literature and Art in the Catholic University, when he lectured on Chaucer; he later published an article on this poet. The next year, 1865, was particularly auspicious for him. He took an MA from the University of Dublin and, after twenty years of legal practice, he took silk, becoming a Queen's Counsel. Most important of all, in that same year he got married.

---

124 *Freeman's Journal*, 13 November 1890, p. 5. Thomas MacNevin (1814–1848) was a prominent Young Irelander and a writer in *The Nation*. He died in sad circumstances in a Bristol asylum (Wikipedia).

Adapting to Married Life

For John O'Hagan to embark on marriage at the age of forty-three was a big step. A long-time bachelor, he was no longer the athletic youth of the 1840s, but a middle-aged man with a receding hairline. Marriage involved entering into a new phase of life, requiring close links with his wife's family. The change required was all the greater since the woman he married was some twenty years his junior. She did, however, come from a similar legal background, and no doubt shared some of his interests.

Frances O'Hagan – no relation of John's – was the younger daughter of Thomas O'Hagan QC, who had been appointed Attorney General for Ireland by Prime Minister Gladstone in 1861. There were three children in the family: Charles, who died young, and two daughters, Madeleine and Frances. How and when John met Frances is not recorded, but in order to consider marriage there must have been opportunities for him to come to know her well. Before approaching her father for permission to marry, he must also have realised that his regard for her was reciprocated. The decisive factors in her father's approval of the marriage, apart from his daughter's wishes, were likely to be O'Hagan's reputation as a lawyer, his financial capacity to keep his daughter in the comfortable lifestyle to which she was accustomed, and his reputation as a kind man and a good Catholic.

As regards Frances herself, little is recorded. There is no pen-portrait of her, apart from some passing comments describing her as a quiet person of considerable kindness and charm, who was deeply committed to her religion without being assertive about it. Her Italian friend and nanny, Annunziata Fonduti, spoke of Frances and her sister as having been born 'with utter forgetfulness of self' and of having had a very happy childhood.[125] Frances must have come to appreciate John's kindness, empathy and absence of self-regard, as well as his spiritual values, which resonated with her own. She was greatly admired by her husband's friends, Matthew Russell of the *Irish Monthly*, Charles Russell (President of Maynooth College) and

125 Annunziata Fonduti – Mother Abbess Grattan of the Poor Clare Monastery, Drumshanbo, County Leitrim, 25 November 1909 (archives of the monastery).

the poet Aubrey de Vere.

Frances and John did not have any children, but all the indications we have suggest that they lived happily together. Their friends viewed them as a united couple who were committed to their Catholic faith and, despite their comfortable lifestyle, to strong social values. They owned two houses, one in fashionable Merrion Square in Dublin, the other some ten miles away on the slopes of Howth Head. Glenaveena, as the house was called, overlooked Dublin Bay, providing a striking view of the bay itself and the hills beyond. The O'Hagans regularly invited friends to visit and dine with them and, from time to time, to stay for some days. When John's work permitted, the couple occasionally travelled abroad to Italy, France and the Balearic Islands.

Apart from their legal background, John had several other things in common with his father-in-law. Thomas was familiar with John's birthplace, Newry, having been editor of *The Newry Chronicle* as a young man. A further connection was through Thomas's sister, who was abbess of the Poor Clares Convent in Newry until she moved to Kenmare, County Kerry, in 1861 to start a new foundation. Like John, Thomas was a member of the SSISI, and was its president from 1867–70. It was he who paid Gavan Duffy's public debts, thereby enabling him to emigrate to Australia in 1856. Despite these connections, political matters may well have created some strain between the two men from time to time. Unlike his son-in-law, Thomas was a supporter of the political union of Ireland with Britain, causing him to lose the support of the Irish Nationalist Party. He was elected as a Liberal Party MP for Tralee in 1863.

Marriage inevitably both modified and expanded John's life experiences. His youthful wife brought a new zest into his world, as well as additional occasions for both celebration and mourning. In 1865, the year of their marriage, he and Frances joined in congratulating Thomas on his appointment as Judge of the Court of Common Appeals. Three years later, under the first administration of Prime Minister Gladstone, there was occasion for another major celebration when Thomas was appointed Lord Chancellor of Ireland, the first Catholic to hold the office since the reign of James II in the seventeenth century.[126] Celebrations were muted, however, by the death of Thomas's wife Mary (née Bell) in that same year. In 1870 Thomas's social standing was further enhanced when he was created Baron O'Hagan of Tullahogue, County Tyrone. It was in that year that he introduced the most notable of his major reforms as Lord Chancellor: the Landlord and Tenant (Ireland) Act, which provided for compensation for tenants in the event of eviction. He assumed office as Vice-Chancellor of the Royal University of Ireland after its incorporation in 1880.

In 1871, Baron O'Hagan caused something of stir by marrying again. Alice Mary Towneley was a young English woman, daughter of Colonel Charles Towneley of Towneley Park, Burnley, Lancashire, and Lady Caroline Molyneux, daughter of the 2nd Earl of Sefton. A woman of strong personality, her presence inevitably brought changes to family life, not least by the birth of two sons and two daughters to the couple in the following years. It is not known how Frances viewed her father's remarriage and his choice of wife.

After his marriage, John pursued his legal work as before, and he continued to write, contributing twenty-one pieces in the 1860s to Dublin Acrostics under the pseudonym '0'.[127] He was also busy with the various public positions he occupied, among which was his role as Commissioner of National Education, to which he had been appointed in 1861. As a nationalist, an educationalist and a Catholic, he valued this role greatly. He knew how the national system of education had evolved, and could see for himself its importance for the education of the country's children.

The Origins of National Education

Prior to the establishment of the national system in 1831, some schools for Catholics were in operation in Ireland with the help of bishops and the religious orders, but their continuance was a constant struggle, since no state aid was forthcoming for Catholic education. In contrast, other schools, especially those of the Kildare

---

126 Lord Chancellor was then the highest judicial office in Ireland. The Chancellor was responsible for the official functioning and independence of the courts.
127 Sturgeon and Quinn, 'O'Hagan, John', in *Dictionary of Irish Biography*, op. cit.

Place Society, received substantial government funding. During the 1820s, evidence of proselytising activity in the Kildare Place schools emerged, and a public outcry ensued. In 1826, the Irish bishops, while well aware that their proposals had no chance of being accepted under a Tory government, made their own position on education clear. They wanted a system of education for Catholic children, in which Catholic teachers, having been educated in Catholic training colleges under the control of the episcopacy, would be present in every school.

With a Whig administration in Westminster in 1831, change became possible, and the Chief Secretary for Ireland, Edward G. Stanley MP, produced a plan for state-supported national education in Ireland. In a letter to the Duke of Leinster in October 1831, Stanley assured him that his plan would banish every suspicion of proselytism from the system, and that the schools, while admitting children of all denominations, would not interfere with the particular tenets of any.[128] With the introduction of this new scheme, a board of seven commissioners was established to administer it, two of whom would be Catholics, and the government grant to the Kildare Place Society was withdrawn, leading to its speedy decline.

The scheme had been developed without consulting the Catholic hierarchy, and was clearly very different from what the bishops themselves had envisaged. As the system was non-denominational in principle, they would have no final say in either the choice of texts to be used or the appointment or dismissal of teachers and inspectors. Nevertheless, Daniel Murray, the Archbishop of Dublin, having decided to accept it as the best available option for educating the poor, persuaded the vast majority of the bishops to follow his lead. He signalled his own commitment to the system by personally accepting one of the Catholic places on the Board of Commissioners, with the other being filled by his friend, Anthony Blake, a prominent Dublin lawyer. Thirty years later, John O'Hagan was appointed to this same position.

---

128 Stanley – Duke of Leinster, October 1831, cited in *Reports of the Commissioners of National Education in Ireland* (Dublin: HM Stationery Office, 1865), vol. 1, p. 1.

The National System in Practice

Commissioners were appointed, not elected, and teachers and parents had little say in the system. The primary task of the commissioners was to administer state aid to the local school committees. This aid was to cover a wide range of expenditures: repairs to property and furniture; permanent salaries for teachers; the purchase of books and stationery at half-price; and, where necessary, one-third of the cost of a new schoolhouse, with the building being vested in the commissioners.[129]

In addition, the commissioners 'issued a list of approved texts for use in the schools and made associated regulations for the conduct of the schools. Inspectors were appointed to see that the approved practices were followed. The commissioners published a series of school texts that proved so successful that they were used throughout Britain and the empire'. These textbooks, although not compulsory, were almost universally adopted in Ireland because they were of a high standard, and also inexpensive. Of greatest importance were the six reading books. These formed a logical, integrated sequence of instruction, taking the child from elementary literacy in the early books to fairly sophisticated lessons in geography, science and literature. Unfortunately, attendance was poor in many places, with children frequently required to earn some income to allay the family's poverty. Most pupils stayed only for the first two books, but those whose parents allowed them to stay the course were able to receive the basis of a secondary education if they had competent teachers.[130]

The administration of the scheme involved a large and complicated structure, as O'Hagan quickly came to realise. In its operation, 'the national system of education was both highly centralised and strongly localised'.[131] Each school was under the control of a local manager. In schools that were largely Catholic, the manager was almost always the parish priest, while in mainly Protestant schools the rector, minister or landlord frequently fulfilled that role. The manager's powers

129 Minutes of National Commissioners, 1 December 1833, National Library of Ireland, Ms 5529, cit. Norman Akinson, *Irish Education: A History of Educational Institutions* (Dublin: Allan Figgis, 1969), p. 94.
130 D. H. Atkinson, 'Pre-University Education, 1792–1870' in W. E. Vaughan (ed.), *A New History of Ireland*, vol.5 (Oxford: Oxford University Press, 2009), p. 530.
131 D. H. Atkinson, art cit. in op. cit., *idem*.

were quite extensive. He was entrusted with the daily oversight of the school, and had the right to appoint teachers, subject – in theory, but seldom in reality – to the commissioners' veto. He could also dismiss teachers whenever he pleased, there being no appeal against arbitrary dismissal until later in the century.

In the context of the United Kingdom in the 1830s, the new system was a revolutionary experiment in state planning, management and secularity. Before long, however, it faltered in its secularity. Because of the benefits it offered Catholics and because proselytism was prohibited, the Church of Ireland withdrew from the system. At first, the Ulster Presbyterians too were hostile to the scheme, with the result that several national schools were burnt down, but before long the Presbyterians negotiated terms that ensured their active participation. From the Catholic point of view, the opinion expressed by James Doyle, bishop of Kildare and Leighlin, proved to be prophetic. Writing to Michael Slattery, parish priest of Borrisoleigh and soon to be Archbishop of Cashel, Doyle pointed out that 'the terms setting up the national system of education … are well suited to the particular circumstances of this distracted country'. He then noted how 'the Protestant clergy … have abandoned the field entirely to us and [this] will have the effect of throwing the education of the Catholic youth of the country into our hands'.[132]

A historian notes that, by 1838, a few years after the introduction of the system, 'the government was spending £50,000 annually on some 150,000 children in 1,600 schools, 1,200 of which were managed by Catholics'. He then adds, 'Given the complexity … of so vast a social experiment, the national system functioned efficiently and fairly.'[133]

During his tours in 1844 and 1845, O'Hagan noticed the great benefits national education was bringing to Catholics in the areas he visited. Almost twenty years later, he was proud to become part of this project by accepting his appointment as Commissioner on the

132 Thomas McGrath. 'Archbishop Slattery and the Episcopal Controversy on Irish National Education, 1838–1841', in *Archivium Historicum*, xxxix (1984), p.18.
133 Emmet Larkin, 'The Quarrel among the Roman Catholic Hierarchy over the National System of Education in Ireland, 1838–1841' in *Humanities*, no. 68 (Cambridge, MA: Dept of Humanities, MIT, 1965), p. 122.

Board of National Education. He continued in office for the next thirty years, until the year of his death, 1890.

Love of Literature

Although now without any particular political allegiance, O'Hagan remained a nationalist by persuasion to the end of his life. A prominent and prosperous member of the legal profession, he nevertheless readily admitted his preference for a literary career. He said as much in a letter to his friend MacCarthy, written on 23 July 1870: 'I have been on the circuit for the last ten days and have been very busy on the whole. Oh! what a difference between a literary chat with you and this law-work which (to say the truth) never went quite with my grain, though it has ended in giving me a fair livelihood.'[134]

Right through the 1860s and into the 1870s, O'Hagan kept up correspondence with MacCarthy on a variety of topics. In some of these, O'Hagan offered comments on poems that MacCarthy had sent, while at other times he was at the receiving end of MacCarthy's criticism of his own efforts. At times, he encouraged MacCarthy to write on particular topics. On 22 September 1866, writing from 20 Kildare Street, he suggested that he write an elegy on John Blake Dillon, who had just died. 'I have been thinking a good deal about JBD', he wrote. 'Ought you not to write something on him – as only you could – a tender and lofty tribute to a man so made to be loved? I am very anxious about this.' It was Dillon who had first introduced O'Hagan to the Young Ireland movement. MacCarthy complied with what O'Hagan described as 'a fine elegy'.[135]

In 1869, writing from his address in Gardiner Street, MacCarthy proposed including a poem of O'Hagan's in a new edition of *The Book of Irish Ballads*, which he had first edited a quarter of a century earlier for James Duffy's *Library of Ireland* series. The suggested poem was entitled 'The Old Story' and had been contributed to *The Nation* in 1845 under the pseudonym 'Carolina Wilhelmina Amelia'. Replying on 26 May 1869, O'Hagan began by sending warm birthday greetings to his old friend: 'My dear MacCarthy, I did not know

134 O'Hagan – MacCarthy, 23 April 1870, in M. Russell, 'Poets I have known … John O'Hagan', in *Irish Monthly*, February 1903, p. 61.
135 O'Hagan – MacCarthy, 22 September 1866, cit. *idem*, p. 72. John Blake Dillon was father of John Dillon MP.

this was your birthday. I send you congratulations, not condolence.' He then went on, 'As to poor Carolina Wilhelmina, it is true that age with stealing steps has clawed her in his touch – and yet, if it were offered to her to go back three and twenty golden years, I think she would say with Cicero, *valde recusem*' ('I would sternly refuse'). O'Hagan then added a verse worthy of Wilhelmina herself:

Could I remount the river of my years
To the first fountain of their smiles and tears,
I would not trace anew the streams of hours
Amid its outworn banks of withered flowers,
But bid it flow, as now, until it glides
Into the ocean of the nameless tides.

In the same playful vein O'Hagan went on to say that Wilhelmina had no objection to seeing reproduced the effusion 'of her hot youth when our great Dan was king', and that she would 'gladly call upon you ... to consider the corrections'. He rounded off the letter saying the he was sorry MacCarthy was laid up, and that he hoped to call at Gardiner Street 'tomorrow or next day after Court'.[136]

Several years later, on 28 December 1873, O'Hagan wrote from County Clare, where he had been appointed Chairman of the Court of Quarter Sessions. He began by conveying his sympathy to Mac-Carthy on a recent bereavement: 'I was very anxious before I left town to go out to see you, but I absolutely had not time. I was so very sorry, for I wished to say a word to you – a word of sympathy at least in the midst of all the sorrows that are weighing upon you and which form a burthen almost too great for you to bear. I can only send you the voice of my sincere sympathy and friendship. I wish from my heart you were living somewhere near me, that we might see each other oftener.'[137]

136 O'Hagan – MacCarthy, 26 May 1869, loc. cit. 'Our great Dan' refers, of course, to Daniel O'Connell, the Liberator.
137 It is likely that the bereavement refers to MacCarthy's daughter, Lillie, aged thirteen, who died on 30 September 1873. It was the start of a period of great sadness for the MacCarthy family. Six months after Lillie's death, on 19 March 1874, another daughter, Josephine, died, at the age of eighteen, followed by the death five months later of MacCarthy's fifty-three-year-old wife, Elizabeth (née Donnelly).

He then went on to speak of a literary project on which he was engaged: 'I venture to send for your criticism what I mentioned to you – a version of the '*Dies Irae*'[138] in the metre of the original. I am by no means satisfied with it.' Sending two versions of a particular section, he asked MacCarthy for his opinion: 'Will you (if you think it worth printing at all) give me the aid of your genius both in choosing between my variations and in striking out something better of your own?' He ended the letter by giving MacCarthy an account of his likely movements in Clare for his reply – 'If you write before Friday, 2nd January, direct to Kilrush; then to Ennistymon till Monday, 5th; afterwards here in Ennis' – and by wishing him 'with all my heart a happy New Year – happier than the past – and with kindest regards to all yours'.[139]

The change and development that took place in O'Hagan's life during the 1860s continued into the next decade, most notably in his legal career.

---

138 *Dies Irae* – literally 'Day of Wrath' – refers to a hymn describing the Last Judgement and sung at funeral masses at the time. Matthew Russell in *Irish Monthly*, February 1903, p. 73, quotes Professor George Saintsbury, in his *The Flourishing of Romance and the Rise of Allegory*, as calling '*Dies Irae*' 'the greatest of all hymns and one of the greatest of all poems'.
139 O'Hagan – MacCarthy, 28 December 1873, in art. cit., *Irish Monthly*, February 1903, p. 73.

CHAPTER 10

An Expanding Career in Law

A Major Court Case

John O'Hagan was Chairman of the Court of Quarter Sessions in County Leitrim from 1870–1873. As was the case earlier in County Westmeath, the position gave him judicial status in dealing with more serious breaches of the law, without any formal appointment as a judge. (Minor violations, such as drunkenness and disorderly behaviour, were dealt with in the Petty Sessions under a magistrate.) The Quarter Sessions involved travelling to different towns, as is clear from O'Hagan's 1873 letter to MacCarthy quoted in the previous chapter. His position in Leitrim allowed him to practise as a barrister also, and in that role the most prominent case in which he figured involved a certain Reverend Robert O'Keeffe of Callan, County Kilkenny, in which O'Hagan was the leading counsel for Cardinal Cullen. That he was chosen for this role was itself a tribute to his reputation as a lawyer and his standing as a Catholic.

The case received much publicity and caused deep divisions. Robert O'Keeffe, the parish priest of Callan, had been suspended from office as manager of several national schools by Paul Cullen, the Archbishop of Dublin and Apostolic Delegate.[140] O'Keeffe brought a suit for libel against Cullen, and claimed that his suspension was invalid. When it came to trial in May 1873, the case was largely a parochial, if bitter, affair, but word of it soon spread throughout Ireland, Britain and beyond. Cullen's involvement, and especially the decision of

140 Cullen was appointed apostolic delegate by Pope Pius IX on his earlier elevation as Archbishop of Armagh and Primate of all Ireland. Subsequently, he was appointed, in the words of his friend, Tobias Kirby (Rector of the Irish College in Rome) 'perpetual apostolic delegate' (See Emmet Larkin, *The Making of the Roman Catholic Church in Ireland, 1850–1860* [Chapel Hill, NC: University of North Carolina Press, 1980], p. 143). Cullen exercised this authority within his archdiocese and as a means of making critical comment on other dioceses, with the approval of the Roman Curia.

the Commissioners of National Education to dismiss O'Keeffe from his position following his clerical suspension, complicated the case, and brought in wider issues relating to the issue of Catholic, and especially papal, jurisdiction within the United Kingdom. O'Keeffe's argument, that his dismissal resulted from the Church bringing pressure to bear on the state to follow its lead, was considered so serious that it was taken up in parliament: 'An Irish archbishop was allowed to proclaim the jurisdiction of the pope, a foreign prince, over the queen's kingdom of Ireland.'[141]

In his final address to the jury, the judge referenced one of the antiquated laws mentioned during the trial, claiming that 'there was now no safety for the government or people of this country against the most mischievous bull that could be invented and read out at Rome, save by the statute of Elizabeth'. Influenced by these remarks, the jury found for O'Keeffe, but awarded him only a farthing in damages.[142] The result was later overturned on appeal.

As a member of the board that had dismissed O'Keeffe, the case must have been somewhat embarrassing for O'Hagan. It prompted him to write a substantial article on the case in the *Dublin Review* of July 1873. By that stage, however, he had already made himself available for the Chairmanship of Quarter Sessions in County Clare.

Transfer to Clare

The Irish Times reported on 15 June 1872, 'It is stated that Mr O'Shaughnessy QC has resigned the office of Chairman of the County Clare, and that the following changes will consequently be necessary: Mr John O'Hagan QC, Chairman of the County Leitrim, is appointed to the vacancy created by Mr O'Shaughnessy's retirement; Mr Neligan is to be transferred from the Chairmanship of the County Louth to that of Leitrim; and Mr W. O'Connor Morris becomes Chairman of Louth.' The same issue commented critically on

141 From Earl Russell's *Essays on the rise and progress of the Christian religion in the west of Europe, from the reign of Tiberius to the end of the Council of Trent* (London: Longmans Green, 1873), p. 321; cit. D. Keogh and A. McDonnell (eds), *Cardinal Paul Cullen and his World* (Dublin, 2011), p. 248.
142 James H. Murphy, 'His Excellency, His Eminence and the Minister: Paul Cullen and the channels of political communication during the first Gladstone administration, 1868–74', in Keogh and McDonnell, op. cit., pp. 248–49, and *Freeman's Journal*, 28 May 1873.

the appointment of 'the Chancellor's son-in-law … to the lucrative post' of Chairman of Clare. It was also indirectly critical of Nilligan, 'of the borough of Tralee', being appointed to replace O'Hagan in Leitrim, and of 'a member of the Junior Bar, Mr. O'Connor Morris' replacing Neligan in Louth. More directly, the report concluded, 'We shall shortly have some observations to make regarding these and certain other legal appointments *which have not more astonished the public than they have the profession.*'[143]

Criticism by *The Irish Times* almost invariably provoked a contrary reaction from the nationalist press. *The Clare Journal* of 17 June 1872 commented, '*The Irish Times* is astonished at certain legal appointments recently made, and in Saturday's issue threatens to "shortly have some observations to make respecting these". It is easy to "astonish" our excitable and effervescent contemporary, whose sails are trimmed to catch every breeze, but we are always prepared for "fits and starts" from that quarter.' The *Journal* then went on to list the appointments and to make the following observation: 'Having personal knowledge of each of the gentlemen above named – of their personal demeanour and integrity, as well as of their position at the bar – we can afford to feel astonished at *The Irish Times'* astonishment.' Then, regarding the County Clare appointment in particular, it added: 'As the retirement of Mr O'Shaughnessy is to be regretted, so are the people of this county to be congratulated on his being succeeded by a gentleman of such urbanity of manner, such accomplishments and legal acumen, as Mr John O'Hagan.'

The Clare Journal subsequently kept a friendly eye on O'Hagan's career as Chairman of the Court of Quarter Sessions. Already, on 24 June 1872, it reported that 'we have already heard respected members of the legal profession practising in this county speak highly of Mr O'Hagan's demeanour on the Bench'. Following the passing of the important Ballot Act by parliament in July,[144] *The Clare Journal* reported on 10 October that 'the revision of voters' and jurors' lists for the barony of Lower Bunratty will be held at Sixmilebridge to-morrow before John C. O'Hagan, Esq QC, Chairman of the Coun-

143 Italics added.
144 The Ballot Act (1872) aimed at amending the law relating to procedure at parliamentary and municipal elections. The introduction of the secret ballot meant that tenants in Ireland could vote against the interests of the landlord class with less fear of the consequences.

ty'. A week later, the paper announced that 'a Court of Revision will be held at Tulla on Saturday and on Ennis next Monday'. On 26 October, the legal correspondent for the *Limerick Chronicle* reported a sitting of the Quarter Sessions at Ennistymon before O'Hagan.

That same Clare correspondent of the *Limerick Chronicle* had already reported on 19 October 1872 that 'last night, John O'Hagan QC, Assistant Barrister of this County, was entertained by the solicitors of the county at Williams Hotel, Kilrush. The banquet was got up on a scale of much magnificence, and the usual loyal and appropriate toasts were drunk. It appears Mr O'Hagan is becoming a great favourite since his appointment to the Chairmanship of this County.'

It was a promising start to O'Hagan's tenure, but the socio-political situation was such that someone in his position had to walk warily. Among the people, there was widespread distrust of the law and of the police, the Royal Irish Constabulary. Both had been associated for a long time with upholding laws supportive of the landlords and the governing authorities. Fenianism also had many supporters in Clare,[145] and links with its American counterpart were in place. Nevertheless, for much of O'Hagan's time as Chairman, the county was relatively quiet and prosperous. Indeed, it was probably more advanced commercially and socially – especially in East Clare – than he expected when he arrived.

The Condition of the County

Across much of County Clare, the early 1870s were years of relative prosperity. This was reflected in the more modern dress to be seen and the upgrading of rural houses to town standards, including the addition of more rooms and windows. Mass-produced goods from Manchester, imported by local shopkeepers, were much in demand. Medium-sized towns frequently benefitted from the relative prosperity of the surrounding farming community. Kilrush, for example, in 1871 had 173 shopkeepers and twenty-six public houses.

145 The Fenians were members of an extreme and secret republican organisation, the Irish Republican Brotherhood, which sought the independence of Ireland by violent revolution. Their name derived from an ancient title for armed Gaelic warriors, Na Fianna. They embarked on an unsuccessful revolution in 1867, but continued to be active in Irish politics until the 1920s.

Transport, too, had improved. O'Hagan was able to travel by train from Dublin to Limerick, and onwards from Limerick to Ennis. To other towns – such as Kilrush, Kilkee or Ennistymon – a car or coach service was available, and the roads to the larger towns were in good condition. The advance in literacy was manifest in the availability of newspapers – Irish and English, national and local. In Ennis, papers could be read in the new town hall and in other reading rooms.

Despite this progress, emigration to England and the US was widespread, and money from emigrants was a welcome source of income. Communication with the US during the 1870s was not confined to letters, as there were occasional visits from Irish Americans, usually on political or economic matters. With cash being widely used in commercial transactions, the number of banks was on the increase.

There was a contrast in prosperity and modernity, however, between the east and the west of the county. Generally speaking, the east of Clare had better land and better roads, its people mostly spoke English, and they were better educated and more fashionably dressed. In poorer west Clare, the land was less hospitable, Irish was still the language spoken by most of the people, and there was a lower level of literacy among the population.

Administering the Law

As Chairman of the Quarter Sessions, O'Hagan had the delicate task of administering the law as impartially and firmly as possible, while showing sensitivity to the cultural and political milieu in which he was operating. To judge from the only case known to the author that was heard by O'Hagan, it seems clear that he was determined to administer the law impartially, without favour to persons of prominence and power. The following is a summary report of this case, which was held on 4 January 1875:

> At the Kilrush Quarter Sessions on Saturday, before John O'Hagan, Esq. QC, Head-Constable Mahony, late of Knock station, now Kilkee, was prosecuted by Michael Morrissey, of Kilrush, for damages sustained by alleged false arrest on the 22 October last. His Lordship said it was clear that Morrissey never intended to steal the cheque, and he

would accordingly give damages, the Head-Constable having in this instance mistaken the law.[146]

Land Agitation and Return to Dublin

The years 1877 to 1879 were marked by severe winters throughout the country and, in addition, three successive harvest failures. These factors, along with the collapse of world agricultural prices because of competition from North America, radicalised both agricultural labourers and the more influential class of tenant farmers. 'The former were faced with the Poor House, the latter with eviction', and both with emigration, if they could afford it, as the only alternative.[147]

In Clare, the scene was quickly changing, with the struggle for land gaining significant momentum. Groups of 'moonlighters', composed mainly of young men, some of them members of the Irish Republican Brotherhood, were attacking by night the crops, cattle and possessions of landlords and, especially, graziers who had bought up large tracts of land. In 1879 the Land League was formed by Michael Davitt, giving structure and drive to the quest of tenants for the 'three Fs' – fair rent, fixity of tenure and free sale. The land struggle would soon be taken up by Parnell and the Irish Parliamentary Party, thereby giving it additional force and voice.

During this period, following the County Officers and Courts (Ireland) Act 1877, O'Hagan's title was changed. He now became known as County Court Judge and Chairman of Quarter Sessions. This brought with it a higher dignity and increased emolument, but required the renunciation of private practice. With much hesitation, O'Hagan chose to retire from the life of a working barrister.[148]

Shortly afterwards, O'Hagan's life took another turn. His duties in Clare had necessitated extended absences from his Dublin home in recent years, but that was about to change. The quarter sessions of October 1878 marked the end of his time in Clare and his return to Dublin. It is not clear if his agreed contract had come to an end or if

146 Kilrush, County Clare, 'Notes from 1760–1960 by Senan Scanlan' in Clare County Library. I am much indebted to the interest and assistance of Peter Beirne, of Clare County Library, for information on John O'Hagan's years in the county.
147 Emmet Larkin, *Historical Dimensions of Irish Catholicism* (Washington, DC: CUA Press, 1984 ed.), pp. 109, 122.
148 M. Russell, 'Judge O'Hagan, some notes from his Life and Letters', in *Irish Monthly*, August 1912, p. 428.

he resigned for some other reason.

In that year, 1878, he became a bencher of King's Inns. Benchers were normally senior members of the judiciary, including all judges of the Supreme Court, the Court of Appeal and the High Court. Barristers and others could qualify in recognition of their contribution to the law, and it was presumably on such grounds that O'Hagan was elected. Three years later, in May 1881, he was appointed Third Serjeant-at-Law, a lucrative position without a heavy workload. Given that he was without any particular political allegiance or connections, this seemed at the time to be as far as O'Hagan was likely to go in the legal profession.[149] Unexpected outside factors, however, were to intervene to change his prospects and disturb his peace.

---

149 See 'John O'Hagan', in *Dictionary of Irish Biography*, op. cit.; and 'Judge O'Hagan', in *Irish Monthly*, August 1912, p. 428.

CHAPTER 11

Land Commissioner and High Court Judge

Gladstone and Land Reform

Gladstone's first administration was elected in 1868 with a commitment to bring about justice for Ireland, including land reform. Land in Ireland was concentrated into relatively few hands, many of them absentee landlords. In 1870, 50 per cent of the island was said to be owned by 750 families.[150] English law protected the absolute rights of landlords, so that it was virtually impossible to challenge them regarding the treatment of their tenants. Active agitation for their rights by tenants was met with Coercion Acts, which provided a legal basis for increased state powers to suppress popular discontent and disorder. These were administered by the law courts, enforced by the police and directed against the majority poorer section of the Irish population. The result was distrust in the law and in policing across much of Ireland.

Gladstone set out to remedy this situation. On 15 January 1870, he remarked in a letter to Lord Grenville: 'To this great country, the state of Ireland after seven hundred years of our tutelage is in my opinion, as long as it continues, an intolerable disgrace.'[151] Many land acts had previously come into force, all favouring the landlord. Gladstone's 1870 Act was different: it was introduced to alleviate the situation of the tenants. It enabled them to receive compensation for improvements they made during their tenancy, and provided for compensation to be paid to them for 'disturbance' damage, if they

---

150 Michael J. Winstanley, *Ireland and the Land Question, 1800–1902* (London: Routledge, 2003), p. 11. Cit. Wikipedia.
151 Cit. Wikipedia under 'Landlord and Tenant Act (Ireland) 1870'.

were evicted for causes other than the non-payment of rent. If the landlord was willing to sell, tenants were also given the opportunity of borrowing from the government two-thirds of the cost of buying their holding, to be paid back at 5 per cent interest over thirty-five years.

Gladstone's act was a major attempt at solving the agrarian problem, but it failed. The operation of the compensation clauses was hindered by the complicated procedures required for claiming and assessing compensation, and it was beyond the capacity of most of the tenants to pay back two-thirds of the purchase price of their holding at 5 per cent interest over the specified time. Evictions continued to increase.

By the time Gladstone and his liberal party were returned to power again, in 1880, the distress and agitation in Ireland had grown significantly. At the end of the 1870s, an agricultural depression had set in, many tenants could not pay their rents, and there were multiple evictions. On 21 October 1879 the Land League, formed in Mayo by Michael Davitt to protect tenants' interests, assert their rights and dissuade others from taking the holdings of evicted tenants, became the Irish National Land League, with Charles Stewart Parnell, of the Irish Parliamentary Party, as its president. This marked the fusion of land agitation and nationalist policy. A land war followed from 1879 to 1881.

The League had as its aims the 'Three Fs' and, while it counselled against violence, it did not prevent some members engaging in intimidation, threats and violence against the property and employees of landlords. In response, Gladstone felt it necessary to bring in another Coercion Act, but he was planning to balance it with a new Land Act which would, in effect, concede the 'Three Fs'. The Land Law (Ireland) Act, which he introduced in the House of Commons on 7 April 1881, passed into law on 22 August. A most complex piece of legislation, it was said that only three persons in the House of Commons had mastered it: Gladstone himself, Attorney-General Hugh Law, and T. M. Healy, a member of the Irish Party for Wexford. In Ireland, the Bill was eagerly studied, and among its close readers was John O'Hagan, whose career it would greatly affect.

O'Hagan's Appointment

Reverend Matthew Russell

O'Hagan had long shown concern for the circumstances of poor Irish tenants, which he had first experienced in his youthful tours in 1844 and 1845. At some point before Gladstone's Act was passed in late August 1881, it seems that O'Hagan discussed this problem and the efforts of the Land League with one of the most distinguished members of the English Bar, Charles Russell QC.[152] Some time later, the latter had a fortuitous meeting with Gladstone, resulting in a long conversation that would influence O'Hagan's future significantly. In a long letter dated 2 August 1881, written while he was 'on circuit, Liverpool', Charles Russell informed his brother about this conversation.

Dear Matthew,

Your surmise is quite right about the Chief Commissioner. The now Governor of Madras (Mr Grant Duff) kindly asked me to stay from Saturday to Monday at his country house a few weeks ago, and the Gladstones were also staying there. I had on Saturday a long talk with the Prime Minister solus cum solo,[153] which lasted for three hours, and in which, strange to say, I had the greater part of the talk to myself, and was listened to apparently with an appreciative interest which certainly astonished me. We renewed our talk the next day (Sunday). His power of receiving new views was

152 Charles Arthur Russell (1832–1900) was born in Newry, County Down. He was one of five children: his three sisters became nuns, and his brother, Matthew, became a Jesuit priest and editor of the *Irish Monthly*. He had a brilliant legal career and is generally regarded as the first advocate of his age. He achieved fame as defence counsel for Parnell in the case against *The Times* newspaper (1888–89). He was made Attorney-General by Gladstone in 1886 and raised to the peerage as Lord Russell of Killowen (after his native village) in 1894. In that same year he was made Lord Chief Justice of England, the first Catholic appointed to this role since the Reformation. Always a faithful Catholic, he died in London in 1900, with the full sacraments of the Church.

153 'Just the two of them'.

indeed remarkable. I did not lose the opportunity of expressing roundly the strong opinion I entertain as regards many things in Ireland, particularly its Executive and Government Board system of management.

I also in particular ventilated my ideas about the Land Bill, to many of which ideas effect has since been given. Indeed, I think I am entitled to say that in this matter I have rendered real and substantial service – far more than has met or even will meet the public eye. As to the Commission, I spoke very openly, but at the time [Hugh] Law ... was undoubtedly intended to be the judicial chief.[154]

Of my amendments to the Land Bill many have been substantially adopted by the Government; and with one exception the rest have been partially adopted. The one exception relates to the amount of the advances, and the time for the repayment under the Bright[155] clauses.

I feel that this letter is rather a puff of myself, but I also feel that you will like to have it.

My dear Matthew,

Yours affectionately,

C. Russell.[156]

Charles Russell did not elaborate on the nature of the amendments he had proposed to Gladstone's Bill, but it should be noted that the Land Law (Ireland) Act, which was passed shortly afterwards, contained significant safeguards for tenants. Yearly tenants were given the right to sell their tenancy at the best available price. A land court was to be established, to which tenants – or landlords and tenants acting in common, but not landlords alone – would have access for the fixing of a fair rent. A limited fixity of tenure was secured to the tenant, so that the judicial rent was fixed for fifteen years, during

154 Italics added.
155 John Bright was President of the Board of Trade. Already in May 1869 he had proposed to Gladstone that 'tenant-proprietorship might eventually be substituted for landlordship as the solution to the Irish land question' (John Morley, *The Life of William Ewart Gladstone* [London: Macmillan, 1903], vol.2, p. 282).
156 C. Russell – M. Russell, 2 August 1881, in *Irish Monthly,* February 1903, pp. 79–80. Gladstone's appreciation of Russell was later reflected in his appointment of him as Attorney General.

John Henry Newman, 1873

which time the tenant could not be evicted except for breach of contract or failure to pay the rent.[157]

Gladstone's hopes for the Land Commission were high. In his view, the clauses in the Act relating to the Land Court were 'the salient point and the cardinal principle of the Bill'. It was his hope that the Court would inject order into the confused state of Irish social relations, creating stability and reconciliation where coercion could not reach. It was 'a right and needful measure'.[158] Significantly, the first judicial head of the Irish Land Commission to be appointed was not Hugh law, as earlier intended, but John O'Hagan.

Gladstone's high hopes for the Commission were reflected among many Irish nationalists. The fact that the judge appointed to head the Land Court was not an Englishman but an Irish Catholic nationalist and a former Young Irelander made them particularly favourable to the Act, but it also gave rise to assumptions about O'Hagan's future performance. Those who knew him, however, were well aware that he would not put his nationalism ahead of his obligations as a judge, or justify violence.

On Assuming Leadership of the New Irish Land Commission

O'Hagan was raised to the position of High Court Judge. He received many congratulations and expressions of good will, but probably none of them meant as much to him as the one from Cardinal Newman. It came indirectly through his friend Matthew Russell, who had informed Newman of O'Hagan's appointment. Newman

157 P. J. Walsh, *William J. Walsh, Archbishop of Dublin* (London: Longmans Green, 1928), p. 111.
158 H. C. G. Matthew, *Gladstone: 1809–1898* (Oxford: Oxford University Press, 1997), p.195.

replied to Russell in his genuine, if rather formal, manner:

> Of course, the Judge is much in my thoughts just now. I hope his health will stand what must be a trial. But he is in a position as singular and rare as it is high. All judges are, to use St Paul's words, 'ministers of God'; but he, as being brought forward on so great and critical occasion, is essentially and emphatically dispenser of at once justice and mercy. I pray God that the measure, of which he is the representative, may issue in a large blessing to Ireland.

O'Hagan wrote to Russell, who had forwarded the letter to him, 'I return the Cardinal's letter. As you may well believe, I could not fail to be deeply touched by it and by the interest in me which he manifested. God bless him.'[159] Newman's prayer that the measure 'may issue in a large blessing for Ireland' came true in the end, but not before O'Hagan first endured pressures and severe trials.

Reactions to the Act

The initial responses to Gladstone's Act were favourable. Many tenants were prepared to take advantage of it, and the Land League, at its convention in Dublin from 15–17 September 1881, agreed to 'test the act',[160] and to give it a chance. The government then made a serious mistake, undermining this initial good will: on 13 October Parnell and a number of his close followers were imprisoned in Kilmainham Gaol. In response, on 18 October, a 'No-Rent Manifesto' was issued from Kilmainham, and two days later C. S. Forster, the Chief Secretary, rushed to judgement, proclaiming the Land League 'an unlawful and criminal association'.

That same day, the Court of the Land Commission was opened at 24 Upper Merrion Street, Dublin, to be followed later that autumn and winter by the establishment of peripatetic sub-commissions.[161] Despite the recent turmoil, O'Hagan marked the opening of the Court of the Land Commission with an eloquent, enthusiastic and hopeful speech, during which he made use of the words of Alexander

159 M. Russell, 'Poets I have known … ', in *Irish Monthly*, February 1903, p. 80.
160 Moody, Martin, Byrne, *A New History of Ireland*, op. cit., p. 354.
161 Moody, Martin, Byrne, op. cit., pp. 354–5.

Pope to claim that henceforth tenants could 'live and thrive'.[162]

Some years later, when it was put to O'Hagan that the effectiveness of the Land Commission had been greatly weakened by Parnell and the Land League, he disagreed. He pointed out that the Land League had been prepared to give the Land Act a chance. The real mischief had been done, he believed, by the foolish action of the government in incarcerating Parnell and key supporters of the Land League shortly after the Act became law.

There were undoubted drawbacks in the Act itself, especially where it excluded from its benefits leaseholders and tenants who were already in arrears with their rent. The National Land League focused attention on these, and they had a strong case. The historian, Joseph Lee, expressed their grievance succinctly: 'As the land courts established under the Act to arbitrate fair rents immediately began reducing rentals by nearly twenty per cent, tenants naturally flocked into the courts to take advantage of this unprecedented concession. But the tenants most urgently in need of relief, those still in arrears of rent – one-third of the tenants throughout the country, nearly two-thirds in Mayo – were ineligible for reductions. This naturally whetted the indignation of those excluded.'[163] The Land League condemned the Land Commission because of this exclusion and urged tenants not to avail of its services. Parnell, seeing how widespread was the support for the Land League's position, endorsed it in its criticism of the Land Act. Consequently, under a recently proclaimed Coercion Act, he and some of his colleagues were imprisoned for a protracted period in Kilmainham Gaol in October 1881 for 'sabotaging the Land Act'.

Parnell's incarceration led to a major increase in agrarian protests; between October 1881 and April 1882 – the period of Parnell's imprisonment – 3,498 outrages were recorded. The extent of the violence convinced Gladstone and Parnell that an arrangement had to be reached. Parnell promised to discourage agitation and in general to support measures of the Liberal government; in return, he

---

162 T. M. Healy, *Letters and Leaders of My Day* (London: Thornton Butterworth, 1928), vol.1, p. 132.
163 Jospeh Lee, *The Modernisation of Irish Society, 1848–1918* (Dublin: Gill & Macmillan, 1973), p. 86.

received specific assurances that coercion would be ended and that rental arears would be wiped out, so that ineligible tenants could avail of the Land Act.[164]

This agreement, however, left unresolved the plight of the lease-holders, who were not permitted to apply to the Land Courts for a revision of their rents. Their exclusion led to protracted agitation by the Land League in the form of the Plan of Campaign.[165] Agitation became so severe that that in 1887 the Tory government permitted all leaseholders to avail of the courts.

Criticism of O'Hagan

After his death in 1890, O'Hagan would come in for criticism in his role as head of the Land Commission. The nationalist *Freeman's Journal* accused him of bitterly disappointing 'the hopes of the Irish people' and 'weakly assenting to the decisions of his colleagues', while *The Nation* claimed that he failed to deliver 'the long-needed social revolution'. The nationalist MP, T. M. Healy, would later call O'Hagan a 'timid man', fearful of the landlord press and class.[166] The above newspaper comments appeared in 1890, and Healy, writing in 1928, was drawing on his memory or on notes from that earlier time. For this reason, these assessments should be interpreted against the background of that period, when not only was the Land War still in operation, but the memory of yet another Coercion Act – the Criminal Law and Procedures (Ireland) Act 1887 – was still raw. Known as the 'perpetual crimes act',[167] this law led to the imprisonment of hundreds of people, including twenty members of parliament.

Against this background, the High Court judge of the government-established Land Commission was a ready target for criticism. As regards the daily operation of the Land Commission, problems

164 Ibid., pp. 86–87.
165 The Plan of Campaign (1886–92) was devised by some members of the Irish Parliamentary Party in conjunction with the Land League to assist tenants unable to pay their full rent because of a poor harvest. It required the landlord to reduce the rent. If he did not, no rent was paid to him and instead it was paid to the campaigners in support of tenants who had been evicted. The League also practised boycotting to considerable effect. The Plan of Campaign proved a powerful instrument and was supported by some Catholic bishops, but was eventually condemned by Rome for its boycotting and no-rent policies.
166 Healy, op. cit., vol. 1, p. 132.
167 Unlike other acts, it did not have to be renewed yearly. It was widely criticised, even by the Irish bishops.

were undoubtedly present: there were inconsistencies in the administration of the courts, contentious and unnecessary appeals were
made, and various other sources of complaint were issued. Healy,
however, can hardly be viewed as objective in his view. He showed
himself venomous towards the landlord class many times in his career, predicting in October 1887, with no little relish, that 'the time
won't be far distant' when he could give glory to God to 'see the big
houses empty, untenanted, and rotting'.[168]

As regards the charge of 'timidity', Healy argued that O'Hagan's
claim in his opening address, that the tenant could 'live and thrive'
in the future, 'was assailed so savagely by the landlord press that he
never recovered from the shock'. In Healy's view, Gladstone too was
fearful of the landlord press, arguing that his omission of leaseholders
from his 1881 Land Act was due to fear of them and of the House of
Lords, and fear also of taunts about the 'violation of contracts'. Some
landlords, indeed, had 'contracts' drawn up with Irish-speaking tenants which were fraudulently constructed to suit the landlord. Healy
provided a case in point: 'When the cottiers in White's Glengariff
estate went into court, documents purporting to be "agreements for
a lease" were put in evidence against them. The watermark of the paper on which they were engrossed showed that it was manufactured
years after the date affixed to the supposed "agreements".' Healy
then mentions the role that O'Hagan played in the case: 'My brother
(Maurice) exposed their spurious nature and Judge O'Hagan rejected them. Yet he refused to impound the forgeries or submit them to
the Attorney-General for the prosecution of the landlord.'[169]

Such inaction on O'Hagan's part encouraged Healy in his view
that he was reluctant to face the landlord press and class out of fear.
In the context of Healy's vituperative eloquence towards opponents
and his aptitude for the rhetoric of affront, the following description
of O'Hagan might almost be considered benign: 'A timid man, but
an excellent poet (translator of the Chanson de Roland and author
of that lovely croon "*The Old Story*").'[170]

Despite the turmoil of the 1880s and the criticism that followed,

168 *Freeman's Journal,* 10 October 1887, cit. Frank Callanan, *T. M. Healy* (Cork: Cork Uni-
     versity Press, 1996), p. 215.
169 Healy, op. cit., loc. cit. Italics added.
170 Healy, op. cit., p.132.

O'Hagan, as President of the Land Commission, helped establish a solid foundation and a legal standard for the commission that led to favourable comment on the Land Act of 1881. Healy himself, in January 1887, was able to state that since its enactment the tenant's interest was superior to that of the landlord and had 'become the dominant and genuine interest in the land'.[171] Ironically, this assertion sounds almost like an acknowledgement of the validity of O'Hagan's hope that 'henceforth tenants could live and thrive'.

More than a century later a biographer of Gladstone was led to observe that 'the Land Commission, with the status of a High Court, established a good general reputation for consistent justice', and that 'the Land Act eventually affected tenure in 65 per cent of the land of Ireland and therein permanently destroyed both the absolute power of the landlord and the doctrine of free contract in rents'.[172] O'Hagan continued in office until weeks before his death.

171 T. M. Healy. 'Jubilee Time in Ireland' in *Contemporary Review*, volume 57 (January 1887), p. 129, cit. Callanan, op. cit., p. 215.
172 Roy Jenkins, *Gladstone* (London: Macmillan, 1995) (paperback edition 2002), p. 476.

Chapter 12

The Song of Roland

A Major Work of Translation

As suggested by T. M. Healy's comment in the previous chapter, O'Hagan's name became publicly linked in the 1880s with the great eleventh-century French epic poem, *La Chanson de Roland*. During his time in Clare, O'Hagan had been working with great dedication on a translation of this poem, while – in typical fashion – leaving it aside when he was required to give his full attention to other matters. In 1878, he announced its completion in a letter to Dr Charles Russell, President of Maynooth College.[173] Russell's interest in the work is evident in his reply to the letter O'Hagan had written from Italy:

Dundalk, 10 October, 1878

My Dear John,

Your letters have been a great enjoyment to me, and I am most grateful to you and my dear Frances for them. They are a foretaste of what I hope from our meeting and from our fireside talk over your travels. I am delighted to hear that you have finished Roland. I have no fear as to the excellence of the execution, but I shall not say a word against any amount of 'polish' you may desire to bestow on it.

It was a happy thought to examine the Venice Ms. and you are doing still better in looking at the Bodleian. I look forward to our meeting, which will be very soon …

---

173 Charles W. Russell (1812–1880) was born at Killough, County Down. He entered Maynooth College in 1826, was ordained as priest in 1835, and became president of the college in 1857. He had a distinguished career, wrote on a variety of topics, and was involved in the conversion of John Henry Newman. He was a founding member of the Historical Manuscripts Commission (1869) and a trustee of The National Library of Ireland (1877). He never fully recovered from a fall from a horse in 1877, and died on 26 February 1880 at John O'Hagan's home.

With best love to my dear F., your ever affectionate friend,
C. W. Russell.[174]

O'Hagan's translation was published in 1880, with a dedication to
Charles Russell, 'without whose interest in it, his advice and schol-
arly criticism, I would never have ventured to publish it'. Russell,
however, did not live to see the publication of the poem and the
wide acclaim that followed. He died in Glenaveena on 26 February
of that year, the recipient of his friend's hospitality and friendship to
the end.

La Chanson de Roland recalls Charlemagne's incursion into Spain
in the second half of the eighth century.[175] As King of the Franks and
declared protector of the papacy, Charlemagne's intention was to engage the Muslim forces that had occupied Spain. The poem is set in
778 during the Battle of Roncevaux (or Roncesvalles) Pass, when
the rearguard of Charlemagne's army, led by his nephew Roland, was
ambushed by Saracen forces, and Roland was killed.[176]

The poem, which had dropped out of sight for centuries until
manuscripts were discovered in 1832 and 1835, was published in
1837. O'Hagan's was the first translation into English. In addition
to translating the original in 'mixed iambic and anapaestic metre', he
also provided a much-praised introduction which located the poem
in its historical setting. He imagined its original reception: the excitement of the crowds in a medieval marketplace as they listened to
a newly arrived jongleur telling the tale, or the delighted residents of
a medieval castle during a 'long and weary evening … when fortune
brought a minstrel who was master of the chansons de geste and,
above all, of the great Song of Roncesvalles'.[177]

The Song of Roland is a very long poem in three parts, with many

---

174 In Matthew Russell, 'O'Hagan's "Song of Roland" and its private critics', in *Irish Monthly,* October 1907, p. 512.
175 Charlemagne, 768–814, became emperor of much of western and central Europe from AD
800.
176 At the time of the battle, the term 'Saracen' referred to Arab Muslims fighting for the
Muslim cause. By the eleventh century, when the poem was composed, it had become
generally interchangeable with 'Muslim'.
177 M. Russell, 'O'Hagan's Song of Roland', in *Irish Monthly,* August 1880, pp. 423–25.
Much of the information on O'Hagan's *Song of Roland* is from Russell's articles in the
Irish Monthly.

characters depicted vividly and distinctly. The central figure is, of course, Roland, who 'is in the prime and strength of youth, the bright, consummate flower of Frankish chivalry'. His great friend is Olivier and, as O'Hagan observes in his introduction, there 'are few things in poetry more touching than the passage where Olivier, wounded to death and blinded by the blood that streams down his forehead, strikes out darkly and smites the helmet of Roland who had ridden to his side':

> Roland marvelled at such a blow,
> And thus bespoke him soft and low:
>   'Hast thou done it, my comrade, wittingly?
> Roland, who loves thee so dear, am I,
> Thou hast no quarrel with me to seek.'
> Olivier answered, 'I hear thee speak,
> But I see thee not. God seeth thee.
> Have I struck thee, brother? Forgive it me.'
> 'I am not hurt, O Olivier;
> And in sight of God, I forgive thee here.'
> Then each to other his head hath laid,
> And in love like this was their parting made.[178]

Favourable Reception

O'Hagan's translation of *La Chanson de Roland* was warmly received and favourably noticed by all the literary organs of the time, from the *Athenaeum* to the *Edinburgh Review*. Matthew Russell judged that, in many respects, 'the fullest and worthiest' of these reviews, written with 'a solidity and thoroughness of minute and out-of-the-way learning', was that which appeared in *The Nineteenth Century*. The reviewer, Agnes Lambert, devoted thirty well-written pages to the poem. She wrote about the significance of the translation:

> The great national epic of France ... was a household word in Europe – in Italy and Spain, in Scandinavia, in the Low Countries, in France and Germany – long before the Italians dreamed of a literature of their own, before the Spaniards had their *Cid*, the Germans their *Nibelungenlied*, or the English

178 Ibid., pp. 424–5.

their *Morte d'Arthur* ... Of this noble epic, of this grand old lay so true to nature ... very few Englishmen have any real definite knowledge; and probably we should most of us have remained without it had it not been for the new translation of Mr O'Hagan, which places it within the reach of the idlest to realise his vague ideas of the chivalry of Roncesvalles and enjoy one of the noblest poems of antiquity.

With respect to O'Hagan's English translation, the reviewer went on to say that 'in spite of the difficulties that stood in his way, Mr O'Hagan, on the whole, gives the spirit of the whole so happily that ... we can now study the *Song of Roland* in our own language, and gain a clear apprehension of the nature and influence of the school of French epic poetry which presided at the birth of European letters ... One cannot praise Mr O'Hagan too much for his rendering of some passages.'

Matthew Russell devoted three editions of the *Irish Monthly* to the *Song of Roland* – in August 1880, August 1887 and October 1907 – and to excerpts from numerous journals and papers, from the *Newry Reporter* to Melbourne's *Victorian Review*. He was happy to quote the reply 'to the attack of some Lord Nobody' that had appeared in *The Spectator*, praising O'Hagan as 'known to all not only as a most learned and experienced lawyer with a serene temper and a judgement of rare balance, but as a scholar of wide and liberal culture, a man beloved and respected by all who know him'.[179]

Russell was also pleased to quote a review that appeared in a most unlikely publication, *Vanity Fair*. In what he described as a 'worldly and somewhat frivolous journal that knew nothing of Judge O'Hagan's antecedents or endowments', Russell found the following laudatory assessment:

To a generation which has sorrowful knowledge of the poetry of dyspepsia, this strong and virile piece of work should come like an unexpected joy. Mr O'Hagan has done no literary work that we are aware of before the present venture, but we think that he has now done enough to give him as lasting a reputation as the frivolous mind of man need desire. We have

179 *Irish Monthly*, August 1887, p. 472.

taken the old *Chanson de Roland* and translated it into sturdy English which almost catches the very tone and savour of the original. He very wisely elects to forswear alike blank verse and prose. Had he chosen to do an unrhymed translation, he could hardly have escaped a certain flatness, however accurately and sweetly he might have managed his rendering. But he writes in that mixture of iambic and anapaestic metres of which Sir Walter Scott had the special secret, and he really adds a poem to our language. From every trace of modern affectation he is as free as the innocent songster who made the original poem. With all its extravagance, with all its naïve credulities, the chanson comes out from under his hands as a manly, stirring, fascinating work. The fighting is told of with a frank gusto and a bloodthirsty humour which are very taking. The volume is beautifully bound, and will make a splendid gift-book. Why it is not already known to many people only the publishers can say. For ourselves, we would willingly give the entire works of our five thousand of modern poets for this one volume of strong freshness.

O'Hagan sent complimentary copies of *The Song of Roland* to a number of friends, among them John K. Ingram, Thomas Andrews, John Francis Waller, Aubrey de Vere and Sir Samuel Ferguson, and he retained some of the responses he received. In his reply on 1 July 1880, Samuel Ferguson, a fellow poet and lawyer, wrote a serious appraisal of *The Song of Roland*:

My Dear O'Hagan,

You have, I think, produced a work of real merit. The Lay itself halts and drags uneasily in its first part. The nature, too, and operation of Ganelon's treason are clumsily brought out. But when it comes to the generous manliness of Roland and his peers, it rises to a clear and delightful pathetic power. Your part of the work will, I imagine, do you and us all credit. Your Introduction seems to me a highly attractive, as well as a solid and valuable, piece of criticism. What I chiefly commend in your version is the manly simplicity and purity of the language and its freedom from the tricky affectations of a medievalised vocabulary. It is my opinion that we have among us here the elements of a better school of literature than they have in the over-refined centres of intelligence in England. I only wish that we could act more together and assist ourselves locally.

Yours, my dear O'Hagan,

Sincerely and truly,

Samuel Ferguson.[180]

Seven years later, O'Hagan would pay his own tribute to Ferguson with several articles in the *Irish Monthly*, subsequently published as *The Poetry of Sir Samuel Ferguson*.[181]

Meanwhile, *The Song of Roland* and its favourable reception had caused a stir in Dublin's middle-class society. Indeed, O'Hagan's name became almost identified with the *The Song of Roland*, as T. M. Healy implied in his remark of nearly fifty years later.[182]

A Man of Many Parts

It is not surprising, perhaps, that O'Hagan – a busy and eminent lawyer, a successful translator, and a man of wide cultural interests, profound erudition and high moral standards – would be seen as a latter-day Thomas More. To his close friend and publisher, Matthew Russell, O'Hagan seemed 'a nineteenth-century edition of Blessed Thomas More'. The comparison may have been suggested by the fact that O'Hagan himself had written about Thomas More in the *Irish Monthly* and had contributed an introduction to an edition of More's *Utopia*. The comparison does not hold, of course, when the political influence More wielded, the offices he held, and the manner of his death are considered. Such common ground as exists can be found in both men's commitment to the legal profession, their love of learning and literature, and their deep spirituality.

As already indicated, Russell's high opinion of O'Hagan had been anticipated by Denis Florence MacCarthy in the poem 'The Lay Missioner', written with his friend in mind. One stanza reads:

180 'O'Hagan's *Song of Roland* and its private critics', in *Irish Monthly*, October 1907, p. 559.
181 Dublin: M. H. Gill, 1887.
182 Healy, op. cit., p. 132.

One I have known, and haply yet I know,
A youth by baser passions undefiled,
Lit by the light of genius and the glow
Which real feeling leaves where once it smiled;
Firm as a man, yet tender as a child;
Armed at all points by fantasy and thought,
To face the true or soar amid the wild;
By love and labour, as a good man ought,
Ready to pay the price by which dear truth is bought!

Some years later, MacCarthy's son, Dr Brendan MacCarthy, who had acted as O'Hagan's secretary for a while, wrote to O'Hagan confirming his father's view of him:

By making me your secretary you made happy my father's last year of life.[183] It was a great source of comfort to him to think that I was under the guidance of you, his oldest friend, for whom he entertained so deep an esteem. During the year that I had the pleasure of working for you (if I may call it work) I have had an opportunity of getting to know you very well and I will always remember you as my father described you in 'The Lay Missioner'.[184]

All through his life, O'Hagan sought to live up to his Christian convictions. As a judge, he sought to embody the high ideal that Cardinal Newman had enunciated for someone in that position. In the service of others, he was, as earlier mentioned, a lifelong member of the St Vincent de Paul Society and a contributor to many charities. He and his wife Frances practised hospitality in their home in Howth and enjoyed the conviviality of their relatives and friends. He was, as Russell wrote, 'a man of intense faith and earnest piety, and especially of fervent devotion to the Blessed Sacrament'.[185] He had a small chapel in his house in Howth, where he had the Blessed Sacrament reserved with the permission of the Archbishop of Dublin. O'Hagan's final book, *The Children's Ballad Rosary* (1892), conveys, on a simpler scale, something of his religious devotion.

183 Denis Florence MacCarthy died in 1882.
184 *Irish Monthly*, Russell, 'Poets I have known ...', pp. 68–69.
185 *Irish Monthly*, February 1903, p. 71.

CHAPTER 13

A Genial Host

Distinguished Visitors

As he mentioned more than once in his letters, the law had been good to O'Hagan and his wife. Not having any children, they travelled a good deal when work permitted; Italy, France and the Balearic Islands are mentioned in their correspondence. Frances, however, found no place to compare with the panoramic view from their own home in Howth, Glenaveena.

The O'Hagans regularly invited friends to their home, sometimes for several days, to share the view and take part in stimulating conversations. Among the known visitors were Matthew Russell and, at different times, his distinguished brother Charles; the other Charles Russell, President of Maynooth College; Christopher Reddington, Commissioner of National Education; William Delaney SJ, President of University College in St Stephen's Green, Dublin; and the poets Aubrey de Vere and Gerard Manley Hopkins SJ.

Hopkins at Glenaveena

There are three references in Hopkins's correspondence[186] reflecting the nature of his relationship with O'Hagan and the times he spent at Glenaveena. Writing on 25–26 May 1888 from University College, St Stephen's Green, Dublin, Hopkins began a rather long letter to his friend and fellow poet, Robert Bridges,[187] with a reference to O'Hagan:

---

186 R. K. R. Thornton and Catherine Phillips (eds), *The Collected Works of Gerard Manley Hopkins. Vol. ii. Correspondence, 1882–1889* (Oxford: Oxford University Press, 2013), pp. 937, 942, 962.

187 Robert Bridges (1844–1930) studied medicine and practised as a physician for many years, publishing his first poems during his medical career (1873). After retiring from medicine in 1882, he devoted all his time to literature and poetry, and was made Poet Laureate in 1913. He wrote in many different genres, including verse drama. Bridges drew attention to Hopkins's poems by publishing some of them in 1918, almost thirty years after his friend's death. Eventually, Hopkins became the more celebrated of the two.

Bridges, have at you. Not a low, not a crow, not a bark, not a bray, from either side of us have crossed the Channel this long while. I am presently going gently to crow, but first I want you to send Nero (and anything else you like, but I recommend that) to Judge O'Hagan, Glenaveena, Howth, Co. Dublin, and, if you can spare one, a copy of the paper on Milton's verse, else I shall have to give him one of mine and, what is worse, get leave to do so. He is an interesting and able man, but old fashioned in notions of poetry, especially rhythm; he thought, without a suspicion, that Shakespeare's verse was often very rough, had never heard of the doctrine of equivalence, and so on.[188]

Writing to his mother six weeks later, on 5 July 1888, Hopkins wrote about how he found everything, from his work to the weather, quite depressing. The only positive note he struck was about a visit he made to Glenaveena: 'I spent a few days lately at Judge O'Hagan's at Howth – the kindest people; and their house is beautifully but somewhat bleakly situated overlooking the bay of Dublin southwards.'[189]

The third reference is contained in Hopkins's reply to a letter from a fellow Jesuit, dated 20 September 1888. Fr Francis Goldie[190] had spent some time in the Balearic Islands gathering material for his *Life of St Alonso Rodriguez*, which would be published in 1889. Around the same time, Hopkins himself was writing a poem, 'In honour of St Alphonsus Rodriquez', about this recently canonised Jesuit brother who had spent most of his life as a humble porter in the college of Majorca. Hopkins informed Goldie:

This evening I am going to Howth to spend a day or two with a friend who, as it happens, has visited the Balearic Isles and has the greatest interest in them, has made a hobby of them, so that I may get something of local colour or point

188 Hopkins – Bridges, 25–26 May, 1888, *The Collected Works of Gerard Manley Hopkins*, op. cit., p. 937. Italics added. *Nero* was a historical verse drama written by Bridges. He had also written much on Milton.
189 Hopkins – his mother, 5 July 1888, ibid., p. 942.
190 Fr Francis Goldie SJ (1836–1912) was an English Jesuit friend of Hopkins. He was author of many books, including *The Life of Blessed John Berchmans* (1877); *A Bygone Oxford: A Lecture* (1881); *The Life of St Alonso Rodriguez* (1889) and *The First Christian Mission to the Great Mogul* (1897).

from him.[191]

Perhaps it was Hopkins's conversation with O'Hagan in Glenaveena that led him to wonder, as he does in the poem, how God

> Could crowd career with conquest while there went
> Those years and years by of world without event
> That in Majorca Alfonso watched the door.[192]

As Hopkins and O'Hagan talked about literature, religion and life during that September visit in 1888, neither of them knew how little time they had left. Hopkins was to die from typhoid in June 1889, while O'Hagan died a year later, in November 1890, from an unnamed malady.

---

191 Hopkins – Goldie, 20 September 1888, *idem*, p. 962.
192 From 'In honour of St. Alphonsus Rodriguez', No. 73, in W. H. Gardiner and N. H. MacKenzie (eds), *The Poems of Gerard Manley Hopkins*, 4th ed. (Oxford: Oxford University Press, 1990).

CHAPTER 14

The Final Year

A Busy Start

O'Hagan showed no signs of serious illness in the early months of 1890, and he continued to live and work as normal. He wrote an article for the *Contemporary Review* on the hero of his youth, Thomas Davis, in which he rejected the image of Davis as a revolutionary. He argued that Davis would readily have accepted Home Rule, and that for 'the blind, levelling, envious, anarchic forces which are the awful menace of our time,[193] he could feel nothing but repugnance'.[194] During those same months, O'Hagan was also working on a biography of Joan of Arc, which would be published posthumously in 1893. Then, on holiday in Italy, he completed *The Children's Ballad Rosary*, which Matthew Russell would later fondly describe as that 'pious little book in which this learned and gifted man became as a child for the sake of children and out of devotion to the Blessed Mother'.[195]

On 13 March 1890, O'Hagan wrote a letter from the Hotel della Luna in Amalfi, in which there is no suggestion of any impending illness.

My Dear Father Russell,

I send you by book post 'The Children's Ballad Rosary' at last. It is very far indeed from what I hoped it might be, but still I felt bound to finish it. It gave me much trouble. 'My invention came like bird lime from frieze' – it plucked away brains and

---

193 The disorder of the time in Ireland may well have been the ground for O'Hagan's language. The 1880s were marked by lawlessness, murder, the Plan of Campaign, its condemnation by Rome, Parnell's struggle for Home Rule, charges that he was complicit in the Phoenix Park murders, his divorce case, the split in the Irish Party and so on. Still, it is difficult in hindsight to identify within Ireland the focus of O'Hagan's condemnation of 'the awful menace of our time'.

194 *Contemporary Review,* lviii, 600, cit. Sturgeon and Quinn, 'John O'Hagan,' in *Dictionary of Irish Biography*, op. cit.

195 M. Russell, 'Poets I have known ... ', in *Irish Monthly*, February 1903, p. 83.

all. I shall be greatly indebted for any emendations you may make. You will see that I contrived to dispense with the imperfect rhymes, 'came, became' and 'turned, returned' which you pointed out to me. You would also oblige me greatly by sending them either in manuscript or in proof, whichever you think best, to Aubrey de Vere. I told him I would send them to him, and I should be very glad of his criticism.

We have been enjoying ourselves very much, especially since we came to this place, where we have had beautiful weather, and the scenery is exquisite. At Naples we gave a day to seeing the western 'Conterini' as far as Pozzuoli and Baiae, with which we were greatly charmed, and another day to Pompeii, at which Fanny's imagination was greatly impressed, and my own, too, though I had seen it before.[196] But she avers that not all the scenery ... has shaken her hearty allegiance to the beauty of the view from Glenaveena.

We like this place so much that we shall probably stay some days more, and then return to Naples. We hope to be in Rome on Palm Sunday, or a day or two before, and to stay at the Hotel de Roma, Piazza San Carlo. If you could send me a proof of the Ballad Rosary to that direction, I will return it to you at once, that is if you think it worthy of being inserted with all its imperfections in your May number.

This region is rich in apostles. In Salerno, where we stayed a couple of days, they have the body of St Matthew in a shrine in a beautiful crypt, where we heard Mass, and both of us offered it for you. Here they have the body of St Andrew.

Believe me ever affectionately yours,

John O'Hagan[197]

Illness and Death

The O'Hagans reached Rome as planned, and there Frances met her old friend from Gubbio, Annunziata Fonduti, with whom they spent several happy days. It was only at this point, it seems, that Frances

---

196 'Fanny' was evidently O'Hagan's affectionate name for Frances.
197 *Irish Monthly,* February 1903, art. cit., p. 84.

perceived that there was something seriously wrong with her husband. Many years later, Fonduti would recall Frances's reaction: 'The dread of losing him was so great she gave vent to her grief with me and said "Should he die, I shall die too". Only God knows what she went through.' Fonduti then added that 'this was nothing to what she had to endure afterwards'.[198]

In the months after his return to Ireland, O'Hagan retired from his roles as President of the Land Commission and Commissioner of the Board of National Schools. Despite the best efforts of his friend and leading medical adviser, Dr Cruise, his condition deteriorated rapidly in the following months. He was confined to bed for the last few days of his life, and died at his home in Glenaveena on Wednesday, 12 November 1890.[199] He was sixty-eight years old.

Tributes from Friends

Matthew Russell's main account of John O'Hagan was published in the February 1903 issue of the *Irish Monthly*. He observed that, while 'eloquent tributes to his work appeared in the organs of every class and creed', he was confining himself in that issue to unpublished testimonies. He chose to focus on the tributes paid to O'Hagan by two of his many friends, Christopher Redington and Aubrey de Vere, each of whom had written to Russell three days after O'Hagan's burial in Glasnevin Cemetery in Dublin.

Redington, the Resident Commissioner of National Education, wrote of his friend's outstanding gifts:

> His character was one that was well suited to earn admiration and respect. His earnest and yet unaggressive religious feelings; his sincere patriotism joined to wider sympathies; his literary tastes which did not interfere with professional work – all tended to make him stand out above the ordinary narrow-minded and commonplace mass of mankind.

Redington then went on to recall pleasant days he had spent at

---

198 Annunziata Fonduti – Mother Abbess of Poor Clare Monastery, Drumshanbo, County Leitrim, 25 November 1909. I am indebted to the present Mother Abbess and to the Sister Archivist for this letter and for much interesting information about Frances O'Hagan.
199 *Freeman's Journal,* 13 November 1890, p. 5.

Glenaveena, 'which left on my mind the memory of a great example of both moral and intellectual elevation'.

In his letter to Russell, Aubrey de Vere expressed his shock at the loss of his close friend and his concern for Frances:

> You will easily understand the sorrow, a very lasting one, with which I heard the sad news of the death of our dear friend, Judge O'Hagan. He was a true Christian and a true Catholic; and it would be well indeed for Ireland if she had many more like him. I hope to write a few lines to his devoted wife a little later and when the shock is less recent; but you would oblige me much if you would send me a few lines to tell me how she bears up under this sad affliction. Like him, she is so devout that in time she cannot fail to have, and in a large measure, the one only true consolation.[200]

Russell concluded his article with the valediction, 'I have heard men who knew him intimately, keen judges of character, declare that John O'Hagan, was the best man they had ever known'.[201]

Reactions of the Press

The *Freeman's Journal*, supporter of the nationalist Irish Parliamentary Party, expressed its deep regret as it announced the death of the Hon. Mr Justice O'Hagan. It then gave an account of his life, noting Gavan Duffy's comment that among the Young Irelanders 'people would have recourse to him, next after Davis, in a personal difficulty needing sympathy and discretion'. His verses in *The Nation* were recalled, as was the place he held in the front rank of his profession – until he was appointed Judge of the new Land Court. Stating that it would be uncharitable to discuss this matter at his open tomb, the paper nevertheless went on to say that 'as a Land Judge he bitterly disappointed the hopes of the Irish people, and he weakly assented to the decisions of his colleagues'. Following further praise of O'Hagan as the most estimable of men in all private relations, and acknowledging his accomplishments as a scholar, the piece concluded, 'Ireland will willingly forget that placed in a position which

---

200 Russell, 'Poets I have known …', op. cit., p. 85. De Vere's prediction would prove to be correct, as will appear in the Postscript below.
201 *Idem.*

he was utterly unfitted for, he was a failure; she will only remember his great talents, his high character, his generous charities, and his simple, gentle, and affectionate spirit.'

The Nation on 15 November recalled O'Hagan's passing under the heading, 'The Death of Sliabh Cuillin'. It went on to outline the early years of his career and the verses he wrote as a Young Irelander, observing that 'unlike others of the versifiers of that period, his poetic talent and taste survived the inspiration of the feelings born of the hopes of that time'. The paper noted O'Hagan's defence of Thomas Moore by quoting his rebuke of those critics who found nothing to admire in Moore: 'It has happened now as at other periods, that fashion has for a time forsaken what is essential and perennial in poetry for the worship of artificial and temporary form.' Mention was then made of O'Hagan's work for Catholic education, the time he spent in the Catholic University, and the translation he made of the great French epic, which it claimed to be the work of a true poet. His time as Land Judge was treated with more understanding in *The Nation* than in *The Freeman's Journal*:

> His appointment to the post of Chief Land Commissioner was hailed by many as a proof that the administration of the Act of 1881 would be something new in the history of Irish experience of law and law courts. His first speech seemed to confirm the hopes; but his work disappointed them. How far the failure was due to a lack of strength in battling with intrigue or to the inherent difficulties of the position remains a matter of dispute. His work was to distribute the fruits of a long-needed social revolution according to the rules of nisi prius,[202] and a failure should hardly have been a surprise. One thing must be counted to his credit. He did not fail, when the time came, to justify Mr Parnell's policy of testing the Land Act; and in his evidence before the House of Lords Committee of Inquiry for the unsatisfactory inconsistencies of administration, delay from frivolous appeals, and other sources

of complaint against the Courts, (he placed the blame) on

202 *Nisi prius* was a historical term in English law in the nineteenth century. It came to be used to denote all actions tried before judges.

the folly that locked up Mr Parnell in Kilmainham in the autumn of 1881, when he was about to give the Act a fair and open trial. But those who are most inclined to judge him harshly here are not forgetful of the records of his youth; and to those who knew him within narrower spheres, where character, however, is not less severely tested, there will now come but the memory of an Irish gentleman of unlimited charity, not merely in deed, but, what is more rare to find, in thought and judgement and word.

The Irish Times, traditionally unionist in outlook, confined its coverage to 'the Land Purchase Court' and its response to O'Hagan's death. It noted that Mr Commissioner MacCarthy, leading the Court, deemed it appropriate to adjourn it out of respect 'for the memory of one who had so long been the judicial head of both departments of the Land Commission'. MacCarthy, it reported, found it hard to speak fittingly of O'Hagan, one of his oldest friends, while noting that O'Hagan's career and character were so well known as to require little elucidation. Having said that, MacCarthy nevertheless went on to offer the following personal and perceptive estimation of O'Hagan:

As a lawyer John O'Hagan fought his way to the first rank of his profession by sheer force of character and authority of learning. As a judge, opinions about him differed, but there never was, or amongst honourable men or fair-minded critics could there be, any difference of opinion as to the absolute rectitude of his intentions. To legal learning Judge O'Hagan added grace of culture, varied wealth of scholarship, and brilliant literary power ... But the man himself was far more loveable and more noble than the lawyer or the scholar. He possessed that which in the *Contemporary Review* of last September he ascribed to Davis – what the Italians call *gentilezza* – a graciousness of character and of conduct which attracted all who came in contact with him. Underneath the graciousness was true nobleness – one might almost say sanctity – of life and character.

Finally, *The Irish Times* reported that Mr Bell BL, 'on behalf of the legal gentlemen present', expressed his concurrence with what had been said from the Bench, adding 'his deep regret at the death of one who had been ever ready to assist his younger brethren by his advice and by his learning'.

'The One Only True Consolation'

In the months before John O'Hagan's death, Frances and he had time to discuss plans and arrangements for the future. Since Frances had no wish to live without her husband at Glenaveena, they decided to offer the property to the Jesuits, with one condition: that the Blessed Sacrament be permanently exposed for adoration in the house. On being informed of this offer, the Jesuit provincial, while expressing his gratitude, let it be known that he could not undertake this commitment. The property eventually passed to the Irish Sisters of Charity, who occupied and expanded it over the next 120 years, using it for sisters returning from the foreign missions or on vacation, and for people on retreat.

After John's death, Frances set about publishing his remaining works, *Joan of Arc* and *The Children's Ballad Rosary*, and arranging the sale of their town house in Merrion Square. Then, after long discussion with her spiritual director, Fr Nicholas Walsh SJ, she decided to enter an enclosed Order of Nuns, the Franciscan Sisters of Perpetual Adoration – commonly known as the Poor Clares – in Drumshanbo, County Leitrim. A year later, on 4 October 1898, she pronounced her vows of religious profession, significantly taking as her name in religion Sister Mary Francis of the Blessed Sacrament. A number of witnesses attended the profession ceremony, including Bishop Joseph Hoare, Fathers John Kelly (parish priest) and Thomas Boylan (curate), and three Jesuits who were close to Frances and her late husband: Fathers Nicholas Walsh, Matthew Russell and James A. Cullen.

Frances, as noted earlier, was one of two sisters, each of whom was of a most unselfish character.[203] In the convent, Frances was noted for that quality, as well as for her deep spirituality and humility. Happy in her vocation, she was well liked by the other sisters. She died unexpectedly on 5 November 1909, aged sixty-five years, and was buried in the peaceful graveyard attached to the convent.[204]

203 Annunziata Fonduti – Mother Abbess Grattan, 25 November 1909. Archives of the Monastery of the Poor Clares, Drumshanbo, County Leitrim.
204 Once again my thanks are due to the present Mother Abbess of the Poor Clares monastery, Drumshanbo, for her considerable efforts in providing information and illustrations concerning Frances O'Hagan (Sr Mary Francis of the Blessed Sacrament).